JERRY FALWELL:
Man of Vision

by Patricia Pingry

An *ideals* Publication

ACKNOWLEDGMENT

Excerpt from "God Bless America" by Irving Berlin on page 13
© Copyright 1938, 1939 by Irving Berlin. © Copyright renewed
1965, 1966 by Irving Berlin. © Copyright assigned to Mrs. Ralph
J. Bunche, Joe DiMaggio and Theodore R. Jackson as Trustees
of GOD BLESS AMERICA Fund. Reprinted by permission of
Irving Berlin Music Corporation.

ISBN 0-89542-027-9 595

Published by Ideals Publishing Corporation
11315 Watertown Plank Road
Milwaukee, WI 53226
Published simultaneously in Canada.

Contents

"Righteousness exalteth a nation: but sin is a reproach to any people" (Prov. 14:34).

1

"I Love America"

It is April 21, 1980, a perfect spring day in Charleston, West Virginia. About six thousand men, women, and children are overflowing the grounds of the magnificent state capitol overlooking the Kanawha River. On the capitol steps, a group of young men and women are entertaining the crowd with their singing. A rally is about to begin.

Protest rallies have become an American tradition, as all sorts of people and groups have practiced the First Amendment. This rally, however, is of a different sort. The crowd is modestly dressed; there are no protest signs. The singers are not from a rock group or a country and western group or even from a popular vocal group. The women all have that girl-next-door look; their hair is shining in the bright sun and their long red dresses are clean and neat. The young men have that freshly scrubbed look; their hair is short and

their white suits are pressed. Behind the singers, rows of American flags form a backdrop. The crowd seems to enjoy the singing; they mill about, chatting and enjoying the warmth—both of the sun and of the singers.

Suddenly, a man emerges from behind the group. Dressed in a dark suit, he is tall, trim, and clutches a Bible in his right arm. The Reverend Jerry Falwell has come to West Virginia to conduct an "I Love America" rally. And that is why this crowd of people has traveled from all over the state—they have come to listen, to applaud, and to join with Falwell in the hope of saving America.

West Virginia was the twentieth state capitol visited by Jerry Falwell, the pastor of a very large church in a very small town; and he doesn't plan to stop his rallies short of appearances in all fifty states.

Why is he here? Falwell has come because,

Photo opposite: Dr. Jerry Falwell speaking at an "I Love America" rally.

5

like Jeremiah of old, he believes there is death in the nation, a moral decay, a crumbling society. He is convinced that America is dying and can be saved in only one way. That is if God performs a miracle.

This is why a minister of God stands at government's door addressing a crowd—some enthusiastic, some curious. He is here because he believes this is America's only chance of survival, and he is here because Jerry Falwell has never left things for others to do if he should do them. Standing on the steps of the state capitol, he declares: "I believe America to be a nation founded by our forefathers as a Christian nation and as a base for world evangelization. For two hundred years God has blessed this country beyond all others, simply because here, in our environment of freedom and liberty, America has, more than any nation in history, been allowed to give the Gospel out to a world for whom Jesus died.

"America is certainly not for Christians only. But the Founding Fathers, though not all were dedicated Christians, were dedicated to Christian principles. They had been influenced by the Puritans, the Pilgrims, the Increase Mathers, the Jonathan Edwards, the George Whitfields, and the Wesleys who were putting together the colonies which became the embryo of the new nation. It was their influence which created the contents of the Declaration of Independence, the Bill of Rights, and the Constitution. They created the philosophy of the free enterprise system from the precepts of the book of Proverbs. The godly people of the Puritans and Pilgrims created the concept of freedom of the press such as the world had never known.

"I feel that the Judeo-Christian ethic, the Old Testament and the New Testament, is the foundation on which this nation was built— unlike any nation ever before in history, with the possible exception of the old nation of Israel, which is no more. I, therefore, believe that America is for all—the atheist, the Moslem, whatever—but it is basically a Christian nation and is certainly a nation of the Book, where Jews have found a refuge they've never known before and Christians have found a freedom they have never enjoyed before. I feel America, for that reason, has experienced a fantastic growth and development, rocketing to the success that she has. You are enjoying the greatest standard of living the world has ever known because you happen to live in a Christian nation that God has blessed.

"Yet we begin to see our country, our republic, crumbling; we see a moving away from God and away from the principles responsible for her greatness. We feel, therefore, that it is high time for the people of God to awaken out of their sleep. We thus feel a primary obligation, in these last days before Jesus comes, to call this nation back to God."

Falwell is an independent Baptist, a member of those Christians who have always believed they have a responsibility to their country. But these rallies are not only for Baptists, nor are they confined to Christians. These gatherings are composed of people of all faiths, or of no faith, who believe that the majority of people live their lives based on a moral code handed down from the founders of this country, a code which corresponds to the Ten Commandments. They also believe the government is listening and responding to the wishes of a vocal minority. They want to change that.

"I Love America" rallies are patriotic and pro-family, but Falwell concentrates on what he terms "moral issues which have become political." In general, these issues apply to the three institutions which, Falwell explains, were established by God. "God established three institutions and no more. He established the family in the Garden of Eden; He established the government; He established the church. Today in America these three institutions must be healthy if we are to have a civilized society." And today in America these three institutions

"For two hundred years God has blessed this country beyond all others, simply because here, in our environment of freedom and liberty, America has, more than any nation in history, been allowed to give the Gospel out to a world for whom Jesus died."

are not healthy, and American society is rapidly moving toward an uncivilized, fearsome state.

Disintegration of these institutions is, according to Falwell, the reason America is in trouble. He points to the government as one of the causes for the present problems but believes moral Americans can effect a change in the minds of the lawmakers.

The first God-created institution, the family, is coming under attack from many sides. A government conference has recently defined a "family" as any two persons living together—a definition with which Dr. Falwell is in absolute disagreement, because a family thus defined could consist, not only of an unmarried man and woman, but of homosexuals as well. To a man who espouses the belief in "one wife for one man for one lifetime" and jokes that God created Adam and Eve, not Adam and Steve, this definition is intolerable. Falwell constantly reasserts his commitment to love the homosexual but considers homosexuality a sin and a threat to the family's existence. He reasons: "I'm against homosexuality because it denies the divine order of the home. God created Adam. Then He took Eve out of Adam and brought her back to Adam. He said a man should leave father and mother and be joined to the wife. This was to be for posterity and was to be God's plan forever. One man for one woman for one lifetime. Homosexuality is not only perverted and ab-

normal, but it destroys the uniqueness of the Christian home.

"There are states in these United States that now have legalized homosexual marriages, men with men, women with women, and have permitted them to adopt children. I really cannot imagine that Sodom and Gomorrah had gotten that low, yet somehow we have. And if God allows America to continue, He owes an apology to Sodom and Gomorrah."

Today's family is also in trouble from a burgeoning divorce rate—over forty percent—and Falwell feels this is partly a result of the movement for passage of the Equal Rights Amendment and the growing number of feminists in the country. He believes that as wives and mothers move into the work force, they have less time for their families. Falwell often speaks of his own mother as the fulfilled and full-time wife and mother: "I thank God my mother loved to be at home. She didn't feel she was in a prison. Her family was her delight. She loved to cook three meals a day and keep the house. She loved to see us off to the school bus in the morning and meet it in the afternoon. She loved to meet our needs and instruct us in right and wrong and enforce our behavior habits. I thank God she felt a fulfilled and happy woman."

These are some of the forces working against the family today, but perhaps to Falwell, the most distasteful legalized sin lies in

the act of abortion on demand. This is the subject against which he is particularly vocal and emotional, and again, his reasons come from the Bible. He quotes Psalm 139:15-16 as proof that a life is formed at conception. *"My substance was not hid from thee, when I was made in secret, and curiously wrought in the lowest parts of the earth. Thine eyes did see my substance, yet being unperfect; and in thy book all my members were written, which in continuance were fashioned, when as yet there was none of them."* To Falwell, abortion is murder and there is no doubt that is against God's law. He says: "God created man in His own image and said, 'Thou shalt not kill.' God Almighty implants immortal life to the soul the moment the seed is planted and conception occurs. Conception and life occur simultaneously. The body of the child belongs to the child, not to the mother, not to the father. Certainly to God first, but his body belongs to the child. There is no more helpless form of life in the world than an unborn child. It is absolutely dependent upon someone else for survival, for existence, for the maintenance of life."

A child growing up is dependent upon others for his physical, mental, and spiritual well-being. Falwell believes the complete responsibility in these areas is placed on the parents, and this responsibility extends to the schooling for that child.

An increasing number of American parents see in public schools dangerous influences against which they wish to protect their children. These are influences of a drug society, the teaching of sex education, the use of humanistic textbooks, the expounding of evolution as fact, and an absence of prayer and patriotism in curriculum. These parents send their chil-

Photo opposite: The "I Love America" singers, all students at LBC, provide music at each state capitol visited by the Falwell team.

Photo right: Young women in bright red dresses and young men in their white suits provide a colorful sight as well as a lovely sound at the "I Love America" rallies.

"I believe that God's people, and particularly God's preachers, will be held more responsible at the Judgment Seat of Christ for the destiny of this country than all the politicians of all times combined."

dren to Christian and private schools where they will have daily prayer, study the Word of God, and receive a thorough foundation in basic curriculum.

The continuance and expansion of Christian schools is a subject of primary importance to Dr. Falwell and the one around which the rallies are organized. The Christian school issue embraces all private and church related schools and Falwell advocates a united force. He suggests that all those concerned with this issue put aside their personal differences and work for a coalition to fight for the same purpose. The Christian school issue is one, as he phrases it, "not of theology, but of survival."

Christian schools have grown from fourteen hundred in 1961 to sixteen thousand in 1979 and are increasing at the rate of nearly four each day. Jerry Falwell sees these Christian schools as "the hope for the turnaround of the country, training leaders to take the country out of the bog it is in now."

The conflict between private schools and government results from the regulations imposed on these schools. As Falwell phrases the schools' rights to exemption from government regulations, "We accept no tax money from the state and we don't like the state to advise us on curriculum, discipline, programs, or anything we're trying to do. We don't mind being regulated on fire, health, or building standards, but we can't be regulated with regard to curri-

culum, to philosophy."

Falwell believes that the dangers of the extinction of the family and the increasing control of its children are sanctioned and subsidized by the federal and state governments. The only way to change this is through the actions of the voters.

Government is that second institution created by God, and Falwell is quick to point out that, although it is controlled by God to suit His purposes, citizens have a responsibility regarding it. Jerry Falwell finds himself in the position of being on the opposite side of his government on the issues of abortion, homosexuality, pornography, Christian school freedom, and the family. He often asks, in amazement, "Why should the church have to battle the federal government for the protection of the family?" He then answers his own question: "We have a Congress trying to hold hands with right and wrong simultaneously."

Falwell believes this is the case, because many of today's adults, and certainly today's leaders, have grown up in homes where morality was taught via the television set and the movie theater, leaving them with no clear foundation for determining right from wrong. Today's leaders have attended schools which taught them a humanism which is inconsistent with God's will. It is this humanism which, Falwell believes, impels the government to legalize the sins of homosexuality, abortion,

"We feel, therefore, that it is high time for the people of God to awaken out of their sleep. We thus feel a primary obligation, in these last days before Jesus comes, to call this nation back to God."

and pornography while it continues to restrict the rights of Christians in the Christian schools and the right of voluntary prayer in the public schools. This lack of a knowledge of right and wrong which stems from a humanistic philosophy has resulted in a leadership crisis.

Today's leaders, instead of forging ahead on a concept of doing what is right, falter by trying to take the most humanistic approach to all problems. One result of this philosophy has been a weakening of the defense of the nation. To Jerry Falwell, a strong national defense is not a strictly political issue, but a moral one as well. "The Bible says that a husband and a father who does not protect his household is worse than an infidel. I'd like to extend that and say a government which does not protect its citizens is worse than an infidel.

"Freedom is the most basic of all moral issues. We need to demand a strong national defense so our children will know the same freedom we've enjoyed."

The freedom of America is rooted in a defense strong enough to keep the peace and active enough to ensure the freedoms upon which this country was founded. John Winthrop called America "a city upon a hill" for the whole world to see that a country founded upon godly principles can work. Jerry Falwell sees a similar mission for America today: "God has a special plan for America. It is the only logical base from which the Gospel can

be disseminated to the world. It's the only nation that has the young people, the Bibles, the churches, the schools, the resources to do it. God loves the world, and this nation is the only one in a position to help the world, half of which goes to bed hungry every night. But if we lose our freedom, all else is lost."

With a disintegrating family, with faltering leadership, and with a weakened defense, how can America survive? Falwell answers, "Only by direct godly intervention. We need a miracle." Many people, even many ministers, believe God no longer works through miracles. Jerry Falwell, however, has seen a lifetime of miracles and knows that no problem is too large, or too small, for God. But each man and woman has a responsibility, and so does that third institution created by God: the church.

"There are 330,000 churches, 330,000 pastors in America compared to 3,000 in our first year of existence, 1776. If 330,000 churches and preachers came back to the Word of God, began to preach Jesus Christ and Him crucified, began to preach and practice holy and biblical living, we could literally shake this nation to her foundations.

"I believe that God's people, and particularly God's preachers, will be held more responsible at the Judgment Seat of Christ for the destiny of this country than all the politicians of all times combined."

Jerry Falwell is calling upon preachers to

"The Founding Fathers advocated separation of church and state so the state couldn't tell the churches what to do and there could be no state church. That's healthy. They did not advocate separation of God and state; the day they passed the First Amendment, they called for a day of fasting and prayer."

proclaim God's Word and to remind each Christian of his responsibility. He emphasizes that God is sovereign; leaders are not in a position of power except that God allows it. "God established government, and those who rule over us are ordained of God. They may not know it, but we know it and are to pray for them. We need a revival of believing and praying. We should pray for all in authority, for their hearts are in God's hand. Sometimes a leader will do something because God has put pressure on him. God has done this because His people have petitioned Him. That's our connection. That's our power."

Falwell exhorts preachers to preach righteousness and take a stand on moral issues, even though they've become political. He calls on ministers to preach loudly enough that the leaders in government will come to realize that the majority of Americans still believe in the Ten Commandments. To those who criticize the combination of religion and politics, Jerry Falwell responds: "It is not against separation of church and state to speak out or hold a rally. The Founding Fathers advocated separation of church and state so the state couldn't tell the churches what to do and there could be no state church. That's healthy. They did not advocate separation of God and state; the day they passed the First Amendment, they called for a day of fasting and prayer."

And that first amendment, which guarantees all Americans freedom of speech, assures Jerry Falwell that same freedom.

This West Virginia "I Love America" rally is, as other rallies, a blend of patriotism and preaching. It is punctuated by laughter, by singing, and by testimonies from elected officials. The rally ends with a prayer sung by the thousands who have come to the capitol steps. As this heretofore silent majority of moral Americans loudly lift their voices in song, they fervently hope their legislators in Washington hear their prayer: *"God bless America, Land that I love. . . . "*

Photo opposite: The facades of the capitols differ, but Jerry Falwell and his team conduct a rally at each.

Photo above: Carey Falwell, Jerry's Dad.

Photo right: Jerry Falwell with his mother. The occasion was the bestowal of an honorary Doctor of Divinity degree on Falwell by Tennessee Temple Theological Seminary, 1968.

"Honor thy father and thy mother: that thy days may be long upon the land which the Lord thy God giveth thee" (Ex. 20:12).

2

The Beginning of a Visionary

Throughout the history of the world, God has called His people from all walks of life and from all places in the world to perform His tasks. But He never calls them without first equipping them for the task. Today, Jerry Falwell is following his conscience in doing the task for which God called him. From the very beginning of his life, Falwell was receiving the training, literally God-given, for the task he would undertake beginning approximately twenty years later.

As Jacob and Esau, Jerry and Gene Falwell were born twins. Like Jacob, Jerry demonstrated a certain impatience early in life. Grade school and high school subjects came easily to the youngster. He skipped the second grade due to a propensity for all subjects and a peculiar aptitude for math, coupled with the desire to read just about every book he could get his hands on, including, at one point, the

dictionary. Falwell graduated from high school at seventeen as class valedictorian and set off to conquer college.

With the birth of the twins, the close-knit Falwell family contained three boys and one girl, although the twins' brother and sister were eight and sixteen years older than the newborns.

Money was not a problem for them even during the Depression years. The father, Carey Falwell, was well known in Lynchburg as a shrewd and competent businessman who was involved in several enterprises and provided a comfortable life for his wife and four children.

The elder Falwell owned several holdings in the small town and his son calls him "brilliant, very astute, with a marvelous business sense." He would rise at four each morning, get the daily newspaper, read it, eat breakfast, and, by six o'clock, be out of the house and

> *"Today, I remind my children that it may take years to find the solution or answer, but you have to operate from the premise that there is a solution. My dad absolutely refused to accept that he couldn't work something out. That attitude has to be built into you."*

gone to conduct the administrative affairs of an entrepreneur. On Saturdays and during school vacations, his young son would be with him. Jerry Falwell recalls: "From the time I can remember, I would be with Dad on every business transaction until he died when I was fifteen. Dad knew how to plan and he instinctively knew what was going to happen next. Somehow, he'd get an idea of where things were moving, and he'd be there first with the most.

"He was very competitive, very tough, very durable. I have to attribute my own tenacity to my father. He didn't know how to give up or how to quit; he'd die before he'd do either. He couldn't admit he was even close to failure in anything and he was always certain there was a solution to every problem and an answer to every question.

"Today, I remind my children of that. It may take years to find the solution or answer, but you have to operate from the premise that there is a solution. My dad absolutely refused to accept that he couldn't work something out. That attitude has to be built into you."

That attitude was built into Jerry Falwell; throughout his life, he has operated on the premise that there is a solution to every problem. The difference between him and his father, however, is that the elder Falwell sought answers within himself, whereas his son's solutions come through prayer and the help of God. Rev. Falwell explains: "In the Christian life, you have to keep yourself thinking victory and trusting Philippians 4:13: *'I can do all things through Christ which strengtheneth me.'* The difference between this and picking oneself up by one's bootstraps is that the philosophy of a 'self-made man' is a tank that runs empty. There are a lot of people who subscribe to a positive attitude but mistake the basis behind it and say, 'I can do it alone; it's all here within me.'

"Many of the motivational organizations teach people that all the necessary resources are within themselves and all they have to do is tap that well. I don't believe that. There's total bankruptcy there. I believe that what you have to do is learn to tap into the Lord; and although He uses your emotions and your mind, your tongue, your talents, and your abilities, you've got to know that it is He doing it through you, that your limitlessness is in Him and not of yourself. It's only when you recognize this will you really be honest with yourself. That's why Dad ultimately failed and, through heavy drinking, died of cirrhosis of the liver. That's why the Ernest Hemingways, the Marilyn Monroes, and all the rest accomplished such unbelievable things and then were wiped out. They just drained their tanks dry."

From Carey Falwell, his son learned the value of hard work, the necessity of a well-run organization, and the authority of the head of the household. Of this latter quality, his son says, "There was never a vote on any issue. Whatever Dad wouldn't allow, wasn't done."

Parental authority clearly dominated the home, and Jerry Falwell is fond of telling the story of the matter of smoking in the home. A

Photo opposite: Jerry Falwell relaxing on the porch of his childhood home outside Lynchburg, Virginia.

17

meticulously clean man, Carey Falwell didn't like the dirtiness or the smell of cigarettes and, for that reason, never allowed tobacco in the house. His oldest son, Lewis, however, had picked up the habit in the navy and on his first leave home had evidently forgotten his father's preference and authority.

"My brother Lewis was eight years older than my brother Gene and I and had been away in World War II as a sailor. Lewis came back after three or four years of combat in the South Pacific. I figured he was a man by that time. He'd picked up smoking while he'd been gone and I recall with amusement the first meal we had after his return.

"One Sunday at noon, Mom, Dad, and all of us were around the dinner table; and I saw Lewis reach into his pocket and pull out a cigarette. I punched Gene to watch what was going to happen. Just as Lewis struck the match and almost got it to the cigarette, Daddy, who was sitting at the opposite corner, never said a word but just reached over and hit Lewis right in the mouth, smashed the cigarette, and laid Lewis out on the floor.

"Without missing a bite, Dad said, 'Nothing's changed here, Son,' and went right on eating. When Lewis got back up to the table, he gave up cigarettes. We all respected Dad for that because he was very consistent on what he stood for."

The tenacity, the hard work, the self-confidence demonstrated by Carey Falwell had a vital and lasting impact on his son Jerry. Although the elder Falwell died when his son was still young, the training and self-discipline which would be necessary later in Falwell's life had already been ingrained in him. His dad also taught him the consequences of the weakness of a life without God at its center.

One of the temporary residents of Elim Home working in the machine shop.

"I believe that what you have to do is learn to tap into the Lord; and although He uses your emotions and your mind, your tongue, your talents, and your abilities, you've got to know that it is He doing it through you, that your limitlessness is in Him and not of yourself. Only when you recognize this will you really be honest with yourself."

Carey Falwell was a man of contrasts. He was not a Christian until his death, yet he certainly lived by many of the Christian principles, such as honesty, hard work, and family discipline. He never smoked and would not allow it in his house; he was strong and self-disciplined enough to build a small-town empire; yet he allowed a personal weakness to destroy him.

Carey Falwell was a drinker. He never drank to the point that it was obvious to the public, but it was obvious to his family and to his son Jerry who saw his father drink while they traveled together. Today, Falwell recalls this habit of his father: "I believe that watching my father drink in this manner throughout my childhood hurt me, and that is why I have such a hatred for liquor and have never had a problem with it in my own life."

What he does seem to have gained, however, is an empathy with the frustrations and helplessness of the families of alcoholics and an understanding that permanent help for the alcoholic involves a great deal more than simply a drying out process. Shortly after the beginning of the Thomas Road Church, men who knew of Falwell's stand and hatred for alcohol began coming to him for help. At the same time, the church realized it had a problem concerning the alcoholics. After having led

them to Christ, the members would then have no means by which to help them with their daily lives.

In January 1959, the church purchased a 165-acre farm in Appomattox County and named it Elim Home, taking the name from the oasis the Jews came to after their flight from Egypt: "... *for I am the Lord that healeth thee. And they came to Elim*" (Ex. 15:26-27).

Elim Home has become a spiritual healing oasis for eighteen men at a time, men who are willing to come in sober and seek permanent help. The ministry involves the needed counseling and requires attendance at services at the Thomas Road Church. Because Elim Home only takes men who have already decided they want this kind of permanent help, the percentage of change is well over fifty percent. Elim Home is part of the legacy Carey Falwell left his son, for with God, all things do work together for good to those who love Him.

Falwell learned firsthand the results of a life without God at its center, even in a materially successful self-made man; but he also learned to love those who are weak. And he learned by example that those who trust to themselves have only a well that runs dry.

His mother, Helen Falwell, was born in Hollywood, Virginia, a few miles beyond Appomattox. She was one of sixteen children, all of whom walked the five miles to school, three and a half miles to church each Sunday, and worked in their father's tobacco farm in their spare time. Life was not luxurious, and hard work was expected of the whole family. As a little girl, Helen Falwell would go into the tobacco fields and pick the worms off the young plants, receiving a penny for every one hundred worms.

Although Carey Falwell was not a Christian, his wife raised her children by her own Christian principles. Because of his mother's example, her son believes that it is possible for every Christian woman, even if she isn't married to a Christian man, to provide a Christian home for her family. "It takes extra effort and special help from the Lord, which I know my mother prayed for. She was a born-again Christian but operating within the limitations of what she knew, and that is where a lot of people live."

Helen Falwell was an example of the type of wife and mother her son believes is necessary for the hope of this nation's children. He often speaks of the woman's place in today's society as first caring for her family's physical, emotional, and spiritual needs and being available to console and communicate with her children. Falwell sees the woman's role as a traditional one: "God has a special ministry for women that's real and powerful. The woman is not a nobody as some would attempt to make her, for God has placed His women in very responsible and important positions in the world. For instance, when the church was first getting started, God saw to it that there were some women in that first meeting who were doing the same thing the men were doing: they were praying. When our Lord was crucified, He saw to it that the women were there on the

Photo left: Dr. Charles E. Fuller, who was influential in the life of Jerry Falwell. This picture was taken on the twenty-fifth anniversary of Dr. Fuller's radio ministry.

Photo opposite: Services at Thomas Road Baptist Church are televised and syndicated to 390 stations throughout the country and the world.

"I would go to the station at six-thirty every morning, seven days a week, and broadcast this live radio appeal. The cost then was seven dollars for a thirty-minute program. That amount was difficult to raise at that time, but I always felt it was worth every cent."

front lines, loving, serving, and ministering; but on resurrection morn, the women were there first. That is important. God always grants the highest dignity and love to a woman. The ministry He gave to the woman is important and it's found first of all in prayer and service to her family. Being a wife and mother is a full-time job, a special God-given responsibility and certainly a very important one."

Helen Falwell was always found at home tending to her responsibilities of preparing the meals, cleaning the house and clothes, and greeting her children when they came home from school. The closeness that existed between mother and son continued throughout her life. Jerry Falwell took the time to show his appreciation to her even after he was married and had a family of his own, and he recalls his mother fondly: "I never saw my Mom become angry or lose her temper. I never heard her say an unkind word. All of my adult life, twice a week, I would call her before I left the house in the morning, and she would fix breakfast for me and would have it ready for me when I got there."

No doubt Helen Falwell's responsible care has a lot to do with her son's advice to today's women to stay in their homes and raise their families, and thus instill the necessary and spiritual qualities in their children at an early age. He recognizes and gives credit for the contributions of his mother to his own life. Falwell may have inherited his drive for excellence and learned the techniques of business from his father, but he garnered his moral standards and spiritual foundation from his mother. He is acutely aware of this fact.

"I owe all my character to my mother; there's no question about that. I owe everything I know about right and wrong to her. I believe a person is molded by the time he is seven or eight, and my mother certainly molded me by constantly guiding me and always being home when I needed her. My mother was driving moral standards into me and indelibly imprint-ing on my mind the importance of honesty, character, morality, decency, and respect for others. My mother was a very gentle woman.

"Mom was very authoritative, very moral, very much a disciplinarian. She taught us right from wrong from infancy. Dad never took much time to do that sort of thing, but Mom did; and as a result, we all knew what we could and could not do and what would happen if we violated the rules. Dad allowed Mother to have that kind of influence."

Perhaps her most profound influence on her son came in an indirect way. It was because of Helen Falwell that Jerry Falwell accepted the Lord. The story is often told but bears repeating because it is so much an integral part of him. His mother attended Sunday School every week; when the boys were very little, she took them along with her. As her sons grew older, however, they didn't want to go to church and, since their father would not insist on it, Mrs. Falwell went to church alone. She was a resourceful woman, however, and she knew the character of her sons. On Sundays, she would not leave the house without tuning the radio into the Charles E. Fuller broadcast, knowing her sons would not rouse themselves from bed to turn it off.

Today, psychologists tell us that we can learn while we sleep; Helen Falwell was ahead of her time. Evidently God's plan and Jerry Falwell's subconscious were working. Gradually, at least one Falwell boy began listening to the Fuller broadcasts. He says, "I became very attracted to [Fuller's] preaching. The music was very beautiful and his compassionate and tender appeals were impressive to me. The fact that he had the meeting where there was a live audience also made it all very real to me. This was during World War II and he would ask for hands to be raised for prayer or help and then would say, 'God bless you, sailor boy.' It was during wartime when I first started listening to him, and I suppose it was because of him that in 1952, listening to him

"I owe all my character to my mother; there's no question about that. I owe everything I know about right and wrong to her. I believe a person is molded by the time he is seven or eight, and my mother certainly molded me by constantly guiding me and always being home when I needed her."

still, but now by choice, I became convinced I needed what he was preaching."

Later, when Falwell began his own church, he immediately started his own radio broadcasts in the belief that, as he was saved through a radio ministry, so could others be. "I would go to the station at six-thirty every morning, seven days a week, and broadcast this live radio appeal. The cost then was seven dollars for a thirty-minute program. That amount was difficult to raise at that time, but I always felt it was worth every cent."

Helen Falwell was probably the greatest supporter of those media broadcasts, because she, too, felt they were worth every cent. Because of the broadcast, her son was in essence "with her" at her death. He tells of this time.

"Mother had stopped coming out on Sunday nights; and during the last few months, she even stopped coming out on Sunday mornings because she was falling quite easily. She was home in her bedroom, sitting in her chair, listening to the Sunday evening program.

Sometime during the broadcast, she suffered the stroke which left her unconscious. She lived two or three months after that, but never regained consciousness."

Today, Rev. Jerry Falwell heads a vast network composed of a seventeen thousand member church, a Christian Academy, Liberty Baptist College, a seminary, a large media ministry, a political organization, and a staff of countless people. Falwell did not come to this task unprepared. God gave him a father who taught him the administrative skills necessary for heading a large organization and who was, in part, responsible for his son's compassion for the weaknesses of others. God blessed him with a mother who was dedicated to the training of her children in moral and social correctness and cared enough for their souls to introduce them to the Word of God. And the Lord equipped Jerry Falwell with a quick and intelligent mind which would enable him to accept the Lord's salvation and thereby receive His blessings.

"Be not conformed to this world, but be ye transformed by the renewing of your mind, that ye may prove what is that good, and acceptable, and perfect will of God (Rom. 12:2).

3

Knowing God's Will

Helen Falwell planted the seed of salvation in her son when, during those Sunday mornings she went to church but left the radio tuned to Dr. Charles E. Fuller and the "Old-Fashioned Revival Hour." It was God, however, who nourished that seed.

After his high school graduation, Falwell entered Lynchburg College. Because he had enjoyed writing as editor of his high school newspaper, he briefly considered preparing for a career in journalism. He chose a major in mechanical engineering, however, intending to transfer to Virginia Polytechnic Institute after completing the two years at Lynchburg. This course of study was a natural one for him because of his interest and skill in mathematics and physics and because he had always been intrigued by building.

His old high school crowd was close and Falwell remained its leader, perhaps because

of his 1934 Plymouth with a 1941 Dodge army truck motor in it which would go 100 miles per hour, and often did, or perhaps because Falwell is a "born leader." The group included Jim Moon, now the assistant pastor of Thomas Road Church.

The days were fun filled, but something seemed to be missing for Jerry Falwell. One day he was talking with his friends and asked if anybody knew of a preacher who preached as Dr. Fuller did. One youth asked, "Is that hell-fire and damnation type of preaching?" Falwell responded that he thought so, and the other boy said his mother went to a church like that.

The next Sunday evening, Falwell and Jim Moon went to the Park Avenue Baptist church. The service provided the germination of the seed planted by Falwell's mother. When the invitational hymn was sung, Falwell and

"There are times when you're not sure, but it's obvious you have to do something. Because your heart's right, God will make the something you do be His will."

Jim Moon went forward and were saved. This event did not separate Falwell from his old friends. The old Plymouth was still packed with "the gang"; but on Sundays, it pulled up in front of the church and eighteen or twenty young people rolled out and headed for the pews. Later, many of that group were saved, and today several are in the ministry.

The change in Falwell was immediate after his conversion. He began to lose interest in the engineering course and started to read the Bible insatiably. His thoughts were dominated by the Christian ministry and he spent hours with the youth pastor, talking about his new faith. As he became involved in church activities, he gradually came to understand the love of Christ. Because of his growing thoughts concerning the ministry, he also began asking people how one knows when God is calling him to the ministry; no one had an answer which satisfied him.

Today, people often ask Jerry Falwell the same question he asked others as a youngster. He tells them: "Isaiah 30:15-20 gives, I think, the best explanation for knowing the Lord's will. God gives us the bread of adversity, the water of affliction. He takes us through failure and problems. He bruises us; he teaches us how to pray, how to pray about everything. He teaches us how to be sensitive to all—the teacher, the people, the Word, prayer, and circumstances. Then the last verse says, 'That you might hear that voice behind you saying, *This is the way, walk ye in it.*' It is the voice of the Lord speaking softly. The voice of Satan is very loud. God's voice is soft, and you really

have to tune in to have the sensitivity that tells you *'this is the way.'*

"There are times when you're not sure which way to turn, but it's obvious you have to do something. Because your heart's right, God will make whatever you do be His will."

One Wednesday night, while the church congregation was singing, "Jesus, Jesus, how I trust Him; How I proved Him o'er and o'er . . ." God spoke to Jerry Falwell in a still, small voice, and Falwell didn't have to ask anyone's advice. During the time it took to sing that hymn, he surrendered his life to full-time Christian service. When the singing had stopped, in typical Falwell impatient fashion, he told the pastor of his decision and asked him to recommend a school for training. The pastor recommended Baptist Bible College in Springfield, Missouri, where his father was a professor. Falwell finished his second year at Lynchburg College; but in the fall of 1952, he headed for Springfield and a different type of training.

During Falwell's time in Springfield, God provided not only classroom instruction, but a great deal of off-campus tutoring as well. There was a constant flow of visiting speakers into Springfield to inform the students of things other churches were doing and to expose the young people to great preaching. These visiting preachers would be met in St. Louis, about 200 miles away, and driven back to the college. In those days, Falwell had a new car each year; so it was natural for the college administration to ask him if he would drive to St. Louis and meet these visitors. He was always anxious to do so; and during the return trip, he would listen to these men, absorbing their attitudes, learning about their innermost feelings, and beginning to understand their problems. He recalls those days: "God allowed me the privilege of being near these men. I was picking up their mannerisms, their attitudes toward life, their families, their churches. It was a great help to me to find that these men, as big as they were in my eyes, were very much in touch with the little things. All of these men were people conscious, people centered, people oriented. Their families were their first priorities and then their congregations.

"At that time I couldn't believe a guy that big could have a problem; but they all had problems. They all discussed their problems and worked through them."

Through observing these ministers, Falwell learned that there are problems in God's church on earth. He learned about the personality clashes and theological differences that are inevitable in any organization. He observed how those men could solve their differences, and he soaked up the qualities of gentle leadership: the ability to guide, not force, to disagree, but pleasantly. He learned the value of a human being, of God's child. For three and a half years, he received a practical training which supplemented classroom studies, and he recognizes the value of that training: "It helps today. We have, as every school does, doctrinal issues which we deal with every year. These problems have to be dealt with tenderly and carefully because we're dealing with people.

"As a college student, I watched these men conserve people, correct situations, deal firmly but lovingly. I learned that you can disagree agreeably, that big men can be completely at opposites on an issue and then sit down at the table and eat together and talk about it without any indication of difference between them. Before, I thought if you disagreed with somebody, you had to dislike them and there could be no way you could ever be friends. But through these visiting ministers, I learned that these men disagreed with each other, yet on the surface they were totally unified. It didn't affect their relationship."

Today, Jerry Falwell exhibits the grace and devotion to people he saw manifested in those men. No one ever hears Dr. Falwell say anything derogatory about any person, no matter what the differences.

During his senior year at Baptist Bible College, Falwell was the associate pastor at the Kansas City Baptist Temple, about 185 miles away. He would drive to Kansas City on Friday night, spend Saturday preparing for Sunday, then return to Springfield Sunday night after evening services. This position was another good training ground for a future minister; but up until three weeks before graduation, Falwell still was not certain that God was

Falwell's graduation picture from Brookville High School in Lynchburg.

27

*"I believe all of life is making decisions
and then making those decisions work. . . .
Sometimes you know clearly and sometimes
you don't; but if your heart is right,
whichever door you go through, God will
make it right and make it honor Him."*

calling him to preach.

Two weeks before the end of school, the pastor of the church in Kansas City came to Falwell and said, "I won't be here this Sunday morning and I want you to preach for me." Falwell had never preached before, and the prospect of beginning in front of a congregation of close to eight hundred frightened him. After all, he had chosen engineering in the first place in order to prevent any sort of public speaking. His minister, however, hadn't asked him if he could, or would; he had just instructed him to do it.

Falwell spent two days and nights in prayer concerning the Sunday message and about the Lord's will concerning the full-time ministry. At the end of two days, he put what he calls a fleece, as did Gideon, before the Lord and prayed, "Lord, if you really want me to be a pastor, when I preach Sunday morning, do something in such a way that I will never doubt again."

Sunday morning came, and the young man went to the pulpit before a packed sanctuary. Falwell had feared the crowds; he saw only individuals. He had been afraid of becoming tongue-tied; he found freedom of expression. He had dreaded loss of memory; he discovered the ability to think on his feet. As with Peter at Pentecost, God provided the words and the ability to His chosen instrument. All the qualities a public speaker must have were given to Jerry Falwell that weekend.

When he gave the invitation, God did the "something in such a way" that Falwell never doubted that God's plan included him as pastor of a church. Nineteen people came forward that morning for various reasons. But one old woman, a charter member of the church, was that special one. She told the young associate pastor, "Everybody always thought I was a Christian, but today I've become convinced by what you have said that I've never been born again." To Falwell, those words were the answer to his prayer. This woman had listened to his pastor's teaching and that of other pastors greater in pulpit ability than this youngster. Yet God had reserved her for this moment, for this young man, for the fulfilling of his fleece. Falwell knew without a doubt that God was calling him to the ministry.

As he had done before, Jerry Falwell had waited until he knew something for certain, then he said, "All right, Lord," and he acted. The next week, he resigned as associate pastor, determined to head for the church to which he believed God had called him.

Falwell had come to another turning point in life where he sought God's will. He discusses how one determines God's will: "I believe all of life is making decisions and then making those decisions work. At the point when the decision must be made, there are often two or three doors right in front of you and all of them look appealing and seem to be possibly the will of God. You have to gather all the facts, do the best you can, decide maybe it's this path, and then go that way. Sometimes you know clearly and sometimes you don't; but if your heart is right, whichever door you go through, God will make it right and make it honor Him.

"Many think Paul was out of the will of God when he went to Jerusalem and was captured and then went on to Rome and died. Others would say he was in the will of God because his prison epistles had to be written. It really doesn't matter. He was warned by the Holy Spirit not to go but he went. The important thing was that, because his heart was right, God used what he did to accomplish the maximum glory for Himself. I think the whole of the Christian life is keeping your heart right, making decisions when they must be made, and then making those decisions work."

At the time of his decision to enter the ministry, Falwell thought the site of his church would be in Macon, Georgia. A family whom he had led back to Christ in 1954 lived in Macon, and they had been asking that he come and start a church there. At that time, he believed that if the Lord did lead him to become a pastor, Macon was the place where he should go.

Before tackling the big job of establishing a church in Macon, however, he decided to stop off in Lynchburg for a couple of weeks. He would use those two weeks to rest and see his girlfriend, Macel Pate, the pianist of Park Avenue Baptist Church where he was saved. Something happened, however, on his way to Macon. In Lynchburg, God gradually unfolded His plan, one which differed from what Jerry Falwell had supposed it to be.

Upon arriving home in Lynchburg, Falwell met with thirty-five people from Macel's church, and his former church home, who were interested in starting a new church in Lynchburg. They asked for his help, and he consented to stay an additional two weeks. "I'll give you a month," he said, "and then I'm off to Macon!"

Scenes similar to the one above are repeated daily in the life of Dr. Falwell. His concern and love for the elderly are genuine.

29

Photo above: The Pastor's Sunday School class in the old Donald Duck Bottling Company building, 1956.

Photo below: Mountain View School where Falwell attended grammar school and where the first church service of Thomas Road Church was held.

"Ye shall be witnesses unto me both in Jerusalem, and in all Judea, and in Samaria, and unto the uttermost part of the earth" (Acts 1:8).

4

The Vision of a Church

In 1956, Jerry Falwell, with thirty-five equally determined people, committed himself to starting a new church in Lynchburg, Virginia. The commitment was to begin a Bible-believing, Bible-teaching church. The new church would be based only on the Bible because, as Jerry Falwell has said, "the Bible, since it is the Word of God, has in it all we need to know about doctrine, from the doctrine of creation to the doctrine of eschatology and the kingdom of God. Not only what is past and present, but what is going to be, that is, the future." So on June 21, 1956, these thirty-six adults, armed only with God's Word as their blueprint and literally nothing else, committed themselves to raising God's banner.

The first meeting was held in the Mountain View Elementary School where Falwell had attended his first six years of school. The following week, the members obtained rental of an unused Donald Duck Bottling plant, the site where the present church stands. They cleaned the old building, rigged up a tent for the children, and held their Sunday School and church services. By August, the group had purchased the adjacent lot and $5,000 worth of lumber and nails. By November, when the weather begins to get brisk in the mountains of Virginia, the newly formed church was housed in a building, crude though it was, raised by the members.

Falwell, who had planned on staying only two weeks in Lynchburg, stayed four weeks, then five, then on and on. This was not, however, because of a sudden revelation that this was where he should be; there was just no opportunity to leave. He says of his remaining: "It wasn't any dramatic thing or any clear revelation; it was a gradual unfolding just in time to go from one step to another." His

"I think a man needs to understand early that he isn't in the ministry because of what he is going to get out of it. He's in it for what he's going to give to others and to the Lord. If he'll think that way, the Lord will honor him."

staying was simply a matter of practical considerations. After all, there were people to visit, land to be bought, a building to be raised, and Falwell was needed. But somewhere along the line, he became convinced that God's plan was for him to pastor a church in Lynchburg. And, as ever, he tackled the task with inexhaustible energy and mathematical precision.

As the Bible was the basis for church doctrine, it became the basis for physical growth. Falwell has often said, "Everything we need to know about the Christian life is in this book, the Bible." He began to apply the passage from Acts 1:8 to his immediate task: *"Ye shall be witnesses unto me both in Jerusalem, and in all Judea, and in Samaria, and unto the uttermost part of the earth."*

Jerry Falwell obtained a large map of Lynchburg and tacked it on the wall. He drew concentric circles, with the church site in the middle. The innermost circle he considered "Judea" and he began taking the Gospel to those people who lived within its perimeter. For each circle, he had a listing of every street, the head of every family, and the family's address.

Each morning at nine o'clock, he would begin his rounds, knocking at each door on each house within that circle. When the door was opened, he'd say, "I'm Jerry Falwell, pastor of the new church here; and I just came by to say hello and invite you to our services." The conversation continued, casual and friendly. He chatted about where the family went to church, if at all, asked about the children—their names and ages—and then took his leave with a second invitation to visit the church. The conversation lasted only two or three minutes, but that was all he needed. After Falwell left the home, he stopped before he moved on to the next house and wrote down all the information he had gathered. At night, he transferred the names and addresses to a circular file.

Once he finished one circle on the map, he began working on the next circle, going into "Samaria." Within the first few years, he had personally knocked on the doors of the majority of the homes in Lynchburg and was moving into the "outermost parts" of the city.

Each week, the ladies of the newly formed church volunteered to help their pastor publish a church bulletin which they mailed to all the families Falwell had contacted. On Saturdays, Falwell spent most of the day on the telephone calling those he had visited during the week, saying, "Hello, Mrs. Jones, this is Jerry Falwell. I was by to see you on Monday. I'd like to remind you that tomorrow we have services at such and such a time, and if you and Mr. Jones can come, I'd love to have you do it."

New people who came on Sunday filled out registration cards which were passed to trained volunteers who visited them before the next evening. With the personal visits, the mailed bulletins, and the telephone calls, was it any wonder that by the end of the first year of its existence, Thomas Road Church had 864 attending the anniversary meeting?

Photo opposite: The Thomas Road Baptist Church complex. The large octagonal building in the center is the main sanctuary. Behind it is the Christian Academy. To the right of the new sanctuary is the old church sanctuary, and to its right is the Donald Duck Building, where the first church began.

Today, the basic plan of visitation remains, and the church still shows that it cares about every person. As a result, the church on Thomas Road has grown from thirty-five to seventeen thousand members. Today, students from the Liberty Baptist College, which is partially funded by the church, also help carry on the visitation program begun by Falwell. The young people go out into the area, two by two, knocking on doors, chatting with the people, and inviting the community to come to church.

Just one week after the beginning of the church, Falwell began his media ministry. He was deeply grateful for those early words from the radio broadcasts of Dr. Charles Fuller. In the beginning, Falwell broadcast thirty minutes daily, seven days a week. It was hard work and an added expense for the church, but Falwell knew firsthand how such a radio ministry could change a life. Today, "The Old-Time Gospel Hour" reaches thousands over 390 television stations and 300 radio stations.

During those first few years of the church, every available cent was put back into its growth. Falwell was the only paid staff member, and his job description encompassed the duties of preacher, janitor, song leader, secretary, and carpenter. His pay was very little, but that was not important. In discussing the challenges faced today by Christians in America, he recalls those years, correlating his duties with the attitude necessary in today's pastors and Christian leaders: "The danger to an American Christian is to unconsciously get caught up in the quest for things to the degree that his priorities get mixed up. There is nothing wrong with having things if God can trust you with them, and if they don't hamper or hinder you from reaching the goals He gives you. The problem with the pastors I know, too many of

The front of the new sanctuary of Thomas Road Church.

34

them, is that they come into a work with interests of 'How much am I going to make now?' 'Where am I going to live?' 'What kind of car am I going to drive?' 'How many weeks of vacation am I going to have?' 'What kind of retirement am I going to have?'

"I teach our youngsters to go out and start a church from scratch. Nobody is there to promise you anything. You've got to care for your family, but God will take care of that. That's not your concern; that's His. This doesn't mean that you need to be flippant or careless about it; a young church ought to be paying its pastor before it buys property.

"I earned sixty-five dollars a week the first year I was pastor of Thomas Road Church. I was the only employee and I got eighty-five dollars a week for the next two years. That wasn't because they wouldn't pay me more, but I could live at home and I didn't need the money. I was willing to furnish my own car, work day and night to build up money and get the land, those kinds of things. Later, when I was married, we began to upgrade the salary purely according to the need I had, not as to what I wanted. My wife worked as a teller in the bank until our first child was born; so it wasn't until the church was very strong, very solvent, very aggressive, and very large that I was willing to accept a salary that made me comfortable.

"I think a man needs to understand early that he isn't in the ministry because of what he is going to get out of it. He's in it for what he's going to give to others and to the Lord. If he'll think that way, the Lord will honor him.

"Here I am, riding around in a jet. I don't own it, the ministry does; but I never planned to have one. I live in a large home now. I never would have bought it nor would I have let the church buy it, but a businessman came to town and bought it and offered it to the church as a parsonage. All those things God will take care of if there's any reason you need them and deserve them. They should never be the goal,

and it should never bother a person to give them up.

"I think that the biggest problem that anybody faces today is when he comes into a profession thinking about what that profession will do for him, what he's going to make, what is his ultimate goal, how much is he going to earn. He should think, 'through this thing I'm going to change the world, effectively put a mark on the world through this thing that God has called me to do and to which I am dedicating myself!' "

In the early days of Thomas Road Church, Falwell was the only paid staff member, although there were many volunteers who helped it grow. And they did have a pianist. From the beginning, Macel filled that spot and continues as pianist today. During those early days, she also kept the church's financial records. These were busy days for both Macel and Falwell, and the two weren't married until the church was two years old. They probably just didn't have the time.

Today, the independent Thomas Road Church has its own mission board with over a million-dollar budget and supports other mission boards as well. An important aspect of the outreach program is Liberty Baptist College Missions. LBC Missions is composed of thirteen teams of thirty young people in each team. These are specialized agriculture, construction, education, and medical teams who are sent to such areas as Latin America, Europe, and Asia. For at least two weeks during their training, students of LBC Missions go into the mission field, where they live in the missionary compounds, build villages, teach, and hand out literature. It's an on-the-job apprenticeship designed to either make a missionary or suggest that he or she seek another career.

Thomas Road Church has a wide domestic outreach program also, covering ministries to the elderly, the deaf, the retarded, and, of course, to the young. This latter program is especially dear to Falwell, for one aspect of it

The choir of Thomas Road Church is seen by thousands via the televised services.

combines two of his interests: youth and athletics. The youth program has its own baseball league and plays against teams on other local leagues for the city championship. Church members literally go out into the streets and invite the youngsters to come play ball. One requirement for joining the teams, however, is that the youngster must regularly attend Sunday School. The ball games are fun, the teams are good, and the Sunday School grows.

But Sunday School is not the only thing which is growing. When youngsters are properly guided by a competent coach, athletics is a good discipline and a good character builder. At Thomas Road Church, the faith is never left within the walls of the building; it is taken into the streets and onto the athletic field and the young ballplayers grow into finer Christians and better human beings.

In the twenty-four years since its beginning, the church has grown from thirty-five members to over seventeen thousand, and the programs it has are some of the most exciting and creative in the country. There have been problems and setbacks along the way, but the pastor's method remains the same. He looks to the will of God and then forges ahead, confident that if he is committed to God's work, God will honor him. In response to the question of whether he has ever doubted that he was following God's plan, Falwell answered: "There has never been a time since I became a Christian that I have ever doubted that God was God or that He was able to do anything. There have been times, because of so many pressures or reverses, I have wondered if I really was doing the Lord's will in a particular instance. I have had to learn through the years the fact that sometimes, even when you're doing God's will as well as you know how to do it, everything will go wrong.

"Sometimes, as it says in Isaiah 53:10, it pleases God for us to fail. It pleased the Lord to bruise Christ. Sometimes it pleases God to bruise us. Not to ultimately hurt us, but to ultimately help us. The biographies of most of the great saints through the ages, today included, would show that there have been some very bruising experiences which can ultimately be explained as a schooling from the Lord. If you can look on your losses and your bruisings as schoolings rather than punishments, I think you can come out ahead.

"It's not important what happens to us, but how we react to what happens to us. The will of God begins first with a total surrender to the Lordship of Christ. That must be the time when you're not only born again, but when you make that total commitment to the Lord. For me it happened a couple of months after I was converted, when I really presented myself to the Lord for a lifetime of service. But then it is a process of progressive unfolding of the Lord's will. A process by which, through the Word of God, through prayer, through people, through what others are saying, through uncontrollable circumstances, it becomes obvious that the Lord is directing, the Lord is guiding. Even by getting off course occasionally, we get more solidly on course in the end."

Falwell admits that there have been times when he has gotten off course. There have been those who have criticized his methods and the large budget of his ministry. Jerry Falwell doesn't waste time worrying about what others think of him; he has work to do.

"If a man will just live for God and walk His way through knowledge, through the real facts and through the truth, the just will be delivered. Truth will win out. Christians don't have to spend their time and their lives fearful of what people are going to say about them. You don't have to defend your reputation. If you walk with God, He will defend your reputation. The man who walks with God is indestructible. God's man is indestructible until the day he's finished the work God has called him to do."

Dr. Falwell in the pulpit during a Sunday morning service.

"Therefore shall a man leave his father and his mother, and shall cleave unto his wife: and they shall be one flesh" (Gen. 2:24).

5

The Vision of a Family

"One woman for one man for one lifetime. This is God's ideal for mankind." Anyone who has listened to Jerry Falwell, even a few times, has, no doubt, heard these words. The family is a very precious part of Dr. Falwell's ministry. It is, in fact, part of the hope for the salvation of the world, for a strong Christian family is a prerequisite for the raising of Christian children dedicated to carrying on God's work.

A Christian family begins with a strong Christian man and a dedicated Christian wife, both working together to create a home where God is honored. Jerry Falwell and his wife Macel have created this kind of home. Within their family the faith Jerry Falwell preaches is practiced daily.

Falwell first saw his future wife, Macel Pate, the evening he walked into the Park Avenue Baptist Church in Lynchburg, the same Sunday evening he was saved. He is fond of telling the story of how he and Jim Moon, now his co-pastor, saw two pretty girls that evening and, to each other, claimed them for their own. When Falwell began showing an interest in Macel, her parents cautioned her about this young man who had a reputation in the small city of Lynchburg for being just a little wild. Macel, however, evidently saw the change that God was working in the heart and soul of Falwell. They kept in touch through his school years and on April 12, 1958, two years after the founding of Thomas Road Church, the two were married.

For the first few years of their marriage, Macel continued her job as teller in the local bank. She also kept the books at the newly formed Thomas Road Church, where each Sunday morning and night and each Wednesday evening found her serving as church pianist.

Photo opposite: The Falwell family, 1980.

39

Falwell exploring the future site of LBC with his children (from left to right) Jerry Jr., Jeannie, and Jonathan, 1971.

When their first child, Jerry Jr., was born, Macel resigned from the bank to become a full-time wife and mother. With the births of daughter Jeannie and a second son, Jonathan, the family was complete. Macel believes, as does her husband, that the raising of children is a career to be taken seriously and requires the expertise, love, and discipline that only a full-time mother can bestow. Spending time with each child is not only a joy for the parent but a necessity for the child. Macel makes a priority of setting aside a special time for each child. She might take one child for an outing, perhaps shopping with her daughter; or she might spend an hour just talking with one of her sons. She believes that a pastor's family, particularly, must work at finding time to talk with each other and says, "A lot of times ministers have lost their children because they have time for everyone, except their own sons

and daughters." Jerry and Macel Falwell work very hard to see that this does not happen in their home.

The Falwells have built their family, first of all, on faith in God and then on a love for each other. The children have been taught that, after God, they come first in their parents' lives; and as busy as Dr. Falwell is, most weeks find him home four or five nights because of the jet the ministry provides for his use. This plane has become a blessing for his family, because, if he is within one thousand miles of Lynchburg, he will return home after a meeting or speaking engagement. On those nights he cannot make it back, the children are waiting for his telephone call, which is sure to come, no matter how late it is when he is finally free.

This type of family closeness requires a constant effort on the part of the parents. Each day begins with family devotions at the breakfast table. Both Macel and Jerry Falwell believe in the necessity of daily Bible reading and have found the morning a good time—not only because it's the time when all are together, but it also is the best way to begin the day, for both children and parents. Devotions are kept informal and take very little time. Each person takes a turn at reading a chapter in the Bible; the family then discusses it together, perhaps applying it to a school discussion or relating the passage to a current personal problem. Then there is prayer for God's guidance and help throughout the day. Devotions are regular and relaxed, but necessary for the well-being of each family member.

Jerry Falwell has often said that the home is where children must be taught the basics of how to live and how to learn the priorities of life. In today's society, it is especially important that values are defined in the home. Falwell believes that the biggest problems facing young people today are materialism and hedonism. He says: "I think the whole of American society today is geared toward pleasure. Boys and girls don't like to work for a goal. The idea is simply to enjoy sports or music or a new car or a thousand other ventures; life is just to find a new pleasure, a new kick, a new thrill. That is, of course, why drugs have become such a powerful force today, because they provide a temporary pleasure. The only hope kids have today is to be raised in a Christian home with values and discipline."

His wife agrees that home is where the child learns about God and His standards through regular devotions, serious conversations, and constant observation. Home is where a child gains answers to practical questions, such as those pertaining to music, dating, or sex. Home is where a child learns to forgive

Bedtime prayers with son Jonathan.

41

and be forgiven. As Macel expresses this lesson: "Parents should be able to say, 'I'm sorry; I made a mistake.' This is how children learn to admit their mistakes and ask forgiveness: when they hear their parents admitting theirs."

It is obvious that Macel and Jerry Falwell's children come before both their mother's personal desires and their father's busy schedule. Dr. Falwell has a rule that he will be home for special occasions such as birthdays. But schedules involve many people, and one such conflict did occur. On son Jonathan's birthday one year, Dr. Falwell went to his son and said, "I'm sorry, Jonathan, but I have a speaking engagement on your birthday. I want to make it up to you. I can either give you the honorarium they offer me or I can stay home."

Jonathan looked up at his father and answered, "I'd rather have you, Dad."

Someone took Dr. Falwell's place that night, and Jonathan received the best gift ever bestowed upon a son—his father. And Dr. Falwell perhaps gained the finest gift also: the knowledge that he is a most precious person to his son.

When a man is as well recognized as is Jerry Falwell, his family often finds difficulty in going unnoticed for long, and they find private moments infrequent. The family attempts to guard their privacy, at times, with a retreat to the ski resort of Wintergreen, Virginia, a trip through the country in a motor home, or cheering the LBC football team on to victory. Occasionally, however, the large television congregation of Rev. Falwell intrudes on his family life, and Jonathan has found himself mildly chastising his dad. At Disneyland one year, after several people had stopped to chat with his father, Jonathan issued his childlike reprimand, "Dad, don't be talkin' to every

Photo opposite: Jerry Jr. with his father in 1974. *Dr. Falwell teaching daughter Jeannie how to fish.*

43

"Parents should be able to say, 'I'm sorry; I made a mistake.' This is how children learn to admit their mistakes and ask forgiveness: when they hear their parents admitting theirs."

Tom, Dick, and Harry!"

With so many demands on Falwell's time, Macel has had the responsibility of most of the daily discipline and decisions. That she has succeeded is obvious from the couple's well-behaved and happy children, and her husband is not reluctant to voice his appreciation: "Macel is an excellent mother. I think God equips wives and mothers for the situations into which he places them. Macel is very leadership oriented, very durable. She adapts to situations quickly and, at times, has had to be both mother and father. She is very authoritative with the children, yet at the same time, very loving. For that reason, we've never had any problem of rebellion."

Although Macel at times has had to be both mother and father, she has the blessings of a closely knit extended family. She is from a Lynchburg family, and her sisters, brother, and father live close by. Her sisters are especially important for companionship, comfort, and advice; and she doesn't let a day go by without talking with them or her father.

The closeness of this extended family is such that daughter Jeannie insists she loves her maternal grandfather more than her parents. Jeannie was born on her grandfather's birthday and he took this as a special gift from God. He is the children's only living grandparent; and, to Jeannie, he is very special. From the time she learned to talk, she has insisted that since her grandfather is older than her parents, therefore likely to die first, she loves him the best. When he leaves this world, she will then give that much more love to her parents.

This is perhaps the logic of a child, but voicing a precept of her father. In contrast to the trend of leaving the old people to fend for themselves, Jerry Falwell feels that the older individual has a great deal to give—to the family, to the church, to the children. He believes, in fact, that it is the old people who have the wisdom and the finances to make the future work for the children of today. They are vital to making the family unit a complete and happy one.

It takes a lot of love to make a happy home. But it also takes the teaching of God's Word, constant loving discipline, a great deal of time, and all members working and playing together to make a successful Christian home.

In his work, Falwell sees the results of broken homes and broken lives. He and his wife work hard to make their home what he has said a Christian home should be. "I do not believe it is the will of God for families to be experiencing hell on earth every day and every night. Yet forty percent of American families today are ending up in divorce courts. And many others are staying together only for the sake of the children or for financial considerations. It is my conviction that God wants the Christian home to be the most heavenly thing upon this earth. It is to be the refuge, the protection, the warmth, and the security of all who live inside the confines of a Christian family."

Photo opposite: The Falwell family, Christmas 1976. From left to right, Jerry Jr., Jeannie, Dr. Falwell, Mrs. Falwell, and Jonathan.

*Part of the building boom of Liberty
Baptist College atop Liberty Mountain in
Lynchburg, Virginia.*

"Study to shew thyself approved unto God, a workman that needeth not to be ashamed, rightly dividing the word of truth" (2 Tim. 2:15).

6

The Vision of Youth

The fondness and genuine love that Jerry Falwell has for young people extends from the children to the over four thousand students who attend Liberty Baptist schools. His interest in youth, however, extends far beyond personal fondness. Falwell sees in the youth of today the hope for tomorrow, and the salvation of a nation.

Falwell calls the training of young people the most fascinating of his many duties; and when with them, he tries to keep them informed of his many projects. Speaking of them he says: "Being pastor of the church is my heartbeat; it's my calling. Television and radio are just methods of reaching millions of people at once from this little spot in Virginia. The training of these young people is the most fascinating part of my life. I speak to them two or three times a week, tell them about our latest project, inform them of the problems we may be having. To me, training the young people, helping them develop, guiding their growth, is a way of multiplying ourselves fifty thousand times."

In order to train these youngsters, Thomas Road Church has grown to include Lynchburg Christian Academy (grades K-12), Thomas Road Bible Institute (a two-year Bible course), Liberty Baptist Seminary (the graduate school), and Liberty Baptist College (a four-year liberal arts college). It all began, however, with grade school.

Lynchburg Christian Academy was started when Jerry Falwell, Jr. was ready for kindergarten and his parents wanted him to attend a Christian school. Not finding one, they, and the church, started one. The school expanded and added grades as the children grew and local interest increased. Today, the Academy is a fully accredited school which emphasizes

"When I get to the end of the road, and, say as Paul did, 'the time of my departure is at hand,' unless I've got several thousand Timothys out there, anointed and called and trained and ready for marching orders, my life and my ministry will be ended."

academic excellence as well as Christian training.

Falwell's love and concern for students is obvious and genuine. As he walks through the halls, he calls children by their first names, tugs a little girl's ponytail, and gives a playful sock to a little boy's shoulder. Dr. Falwell obviously enjoys the young children—students in the first phase of their training. Falwell says of these schools, "They are the hope for the turnaround of the country."

Pastors who graduate from LBC are urged to begin schools along with their churches. Already two hundred young men have gone out and started churches on their own; and new churches—and schools—are averaging two or three a week. Falwell sees the number mushrooming: "We will start as many schools in 1980 as we have started in the last two years. The following year it will be four times what we've done. We will start five thousand churches in this decade in North America. In 1988, the real impact will come—in nearly every town, every country, every place, there will our kids be. These schools are a way for a minister to reproduce the Christian life that God is forming in him, by creating it in the lives of others on a regular, almost daily, basis. These schools are the way I see of lifting and turning the nation around. These are the leaders. These pastors who have gone out from LBC are now sending kids back to LBC by the hundreds."

The Christian schools are the means of producing Christian leaders, "Young Timothys" Falwell calls them. But the means of producing the Christian schools are the

churches throughout the country. And the beginnings of those churches lie in Liberty Baptist College—perhaps the most phenomenal college in the country.

LBC officially opened its doors in September 1971 with no campus, no dormitories, no large ivy-covered halls. Like the church begun fifteen years before, the only things the college had were the Bible as guidebook and the vision of Jerry Falwell.

LBC has been described as a "boot camp" for training champions. As might be expected from this description, discipline is strict, the dress code is modest, and dating regulations are enforced. Certain television programs are against the rules, as are smoking, alcoholic beverages, and rock music. Considering the lack of restrictions in most colleges today, a visitor is struck by the attitude of the students. Although they may rebel at first, the ones who stay not only don't mind the restrictions, but would have it no other way. Students at LBC are as serious about their calling as is their chancellor.

That chancellor, Dr. Falwell, runs the school by the same code he believes God uses in training His people in what he has termed the "university of God": "We are called into this school, this university of God. He regulates and disciplines those who are in His schools. One of the great deficiencies of modern-day education is that it lacks one very essential ingredient—discipline. You can attend most of the universities and colleges in America today dressed in overalls and bare-

Photo opposite: Jerry Falwell visits one of the hundreds of Thomas Road Baptist Church's Sunday School classes.

footed, with an American flag attached to the seat of your pants. You can walk in smoking a cigarette, with your hair down and over your ears and with your face dirty, and all is well. No discipline. You can get up when you please and walk around, talk back to the professor, show arrogance toward all civil and religious authority and parental authority. In God's school, there's always discipline. *'Whom the Lord loveth He chasteneth, and scourgeth every son whom He receiveth'"* (Heb. 12:6).

The regulations at LBC are strict, but they are only outward signs of the self-discipline the school tries to instill in every student, for much is expected of these students. To whom much has been given, much is expected; and these students have been given much: eternal life and the salvation of God. They are to be champions for Christ, young Timothys in an evil world, and the hope for the nation's survival.

The short history of this school is rich. Since its founding in 1971, it has undergone growth from rented buildings, donated sleeping rooms, and classrooms on porches to a modern campus, still enlarging, on four thousand acres of lovely rolling land named (or, more accurately, renamed by Falwell) Liberty Mountain. Part of tuition expenses and the cost of the land and buildings are financially underwritten by the thousands of people who follow the growth of LBC via "The Old-Time Gospel Hour."

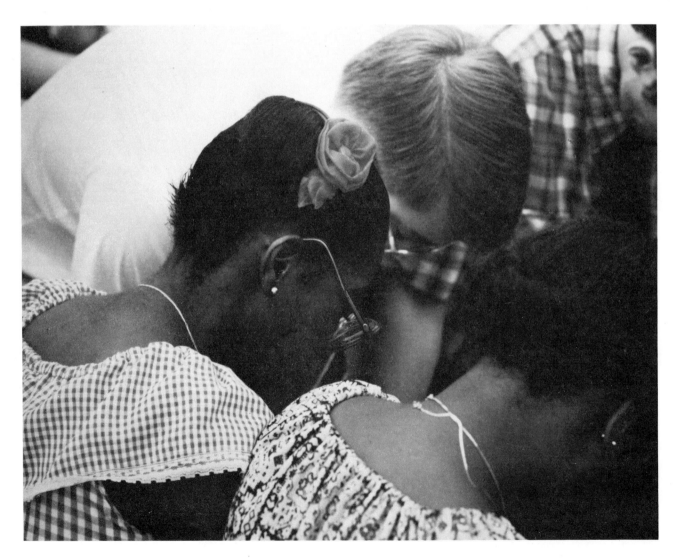

Students of LBC at an outdoor prayer meeting.

Students who arrive at the campus hear of this history. They hear of the time in 1973 when the Securities and Exchange Commission brought Falwell to trial for alleged "fraud and deceit" in the issuance of bonds. They hear that the crisis stemmed from the oversight of not seeking prior governmental approval of the bonds; and they also hear that Jerry Falwell and God won. The church was cleared of wrongdoing but given only three years to pay off the bonds. New students are undoubtedly told that there was a very real possibility that LBC would have to close its doors during that time, but the students sold guitars, stereos, and even took to the road with rallies to help pay off the bonds. And new students certainly hear the triumphant conclusion, "We paid off those bonds in three years."

The entering students also learn that as a result of another crisis, one cold day in January of 1977, the school was losing its rented buildings and would have no classrooms for the fall. Older students and faculty recall the student body standing outside in eight inches of snow on a barren mountain asking God for a miracle to provide buildings for the fall. The miracle they were asking for was 2.5 million dollars to pay off all existing debt and provide money to build on that mountain. And they learn that, to Jerry Falwell, 2.5 million dollars is no bigger miracle to God than $250, for God provided then as he had in the past. And the new students at LBC become convinced that God will continue to provide.

New students are also introduced to their chancellor, Dr. Jerry Falwell, whose personality is stamped on LBC and who is largely responsible for founding the college. He is also the primary person from whom the students have come to learn.

Falwell combines his dream of training a youth corps for God with recognition of the difficulty in attracting the very best of today's youth. And he wants the best young people available; it doesn't matter if they come in wheelchairs or if they are, at first, on probation, as long as they are the most committed, the most brave, the most farsighted. For fulfillment of the vision God has given him, Falwell must have the best.

But the top academic students in today's high schools seek an accredited college. So LBC is working diligently for accreditation by the Southern Association of Colleges. The best students don't attend small colleges with few facilities. So Falwell makes this the *best* small college it can be, with a growing enrollment and buildings rising almost daily. A new library and a modern music building have just been built, and the school offers an unusually high number of doctorates on the staff. LBC may be a small college today, but they have set a goal of fifty thousand enrollment by the year 2000.

Falwell planned a liberal arts college. Although church ministry is the school's largest graduating major and its forte, Falwell is interested not just in training ministers, but in training Christians to serve God in all walks of life. The liberal arts program allows for majors in Christian education (second to ministry in number of graduates), business, television and film, and political science. Among the minors offered is one of particular interest to Falwell, journalism. "Because of the power of the pen, especially in the hand of a Christian, we would like to have a major in this." In 1980, LBC offered twenty-two major courses, and Falwell envisions a school of medicine, law, and engineering, "so that the student, no matter what he wants to study, who wants to serve the Lord in whatever area, can come here for the first four years." This is a visionary basis for what Falwell is fond of saying: "We don't teach students simply how to make a living, we teach them how to live."

Another group of students not forgotten by Falwell are the athletes, because athletes who are excellent students, though they may also be good Christian young people, don't

51

attend obscure colleges with weak athletic teams. Falwell seeks NCAA status with a Division I athletic department. This facet of the school is one of its most fascinating and most public aspects.

There are several practical reasons for seeking Division I athletic status. First of all, as Falwell readily points out, football is a major money-making program which can help all programs. It also adds prestige and distinction to the school, and it attracts young people.

During the 1979 season, the LBC football team beat the University of Dayton, a nationally ranked team, and finished 9-1-1 for the season. On the schedules, LBC used to be a "breather" for the larger colleges. No longer. Now those large universities are taking a second look at this team. LBC's football team is becoming powerful enough that it is no longer an embarrassment to lose to them.

Other sports teams at LBC are just as aggressive. Baseball and wrestling are already competing against Division I schools. The wrestling team in 1979 won their fourth consecutive NCCAA (National Christian Colleges Athletic Association) championship, and the baseball team has defeated every major team in Virginia, including the University of Virginia and Virginia Polytechnic Institute.

There is more than just prestige involved, however, in this fierce desire to bring the athletic department up to Division I status. Back of it all, Falwell is still thinking of the student: "There are a lot of young people who have professional athletics as a goal, and must be sure, when they leave high school, to foster that goal. They must play for a college watched by the pros and one where they will receive national exposure. If a student goes from high school into a college which has a very weak athletic program, it's very difficult for that young man to be seen by the right people. But with a program like ours, as we forge upward, a kid that comes here will be seen as much as if he were playing for Ohio State. And when we

finally become Division I, then there will be no difference. Then we will not be competing at a disadvantage.

"We will really have the advantage then because of the spiritual emphasis. The fundamentalist kid will look on Liberty the same way a Roman Catholic youngster looks on Notre Dame. If he is a superstar and can play for Notre Dame, that's where he wants to go. We want to create the same kind of incentive for the evangelical Christian youngster. If he could play football at Liberty, he would prefer to be here rather than anywhere else. That way, we get the best youngster and the blue-chip athlete. The stronger a school is, the more recognition of its program, the more students of all kinds, not just athletes, are attracted to it. If we are to have fifty thousand students and university status here by the turn of the century, we must have a super program."

The vision of a top-notch liberal arts university which attracts the best students in every discipline, then trains them to go out and train others, is at the same time both complex and simple. It is based on Falwell's belief that if a Christian is doing God's will, he will be the best in whatever field he has chosen. It's based on a desire to change a nation by educating the youth and giving them the tools by which to turn the nation back to God. And, primarily, that vision of training "young Timothys" is based on the Great Commission, *"Go ye therefore, and teach all nations, baptizing them in the name of the Father, and of the Son, and of the Holy Ghost: Teaching them to observe all things whatsoever I have commanded you: and, lo, I am with you alway, even unto the end of the world"* (Matt. 28:19).

Falwell explains that "the promise of God's presence and God's power, God's provision, is upon those and those only who are under the mandate, personally having caught the vision to give the Gospel to the world."

Even in the field of education, Jerry Fal-

Photo opposite: Jerry Falwell joined with six LBC students in prayer on Liberty Mountain.

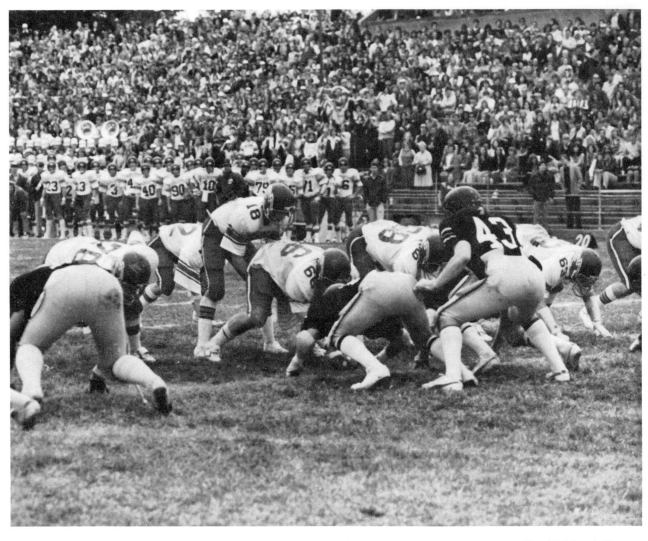

The LBC football team.

well takes his call to the ministry seriously. He is still searching for souls to lead to Christ. Tell the Gospel to a hundred, let them tell a hundred, and soon the whole world has heard the message. "When I get to the end of the road," Falwell says, "and say, as Paul did, 'the time of my departure is at hand,' unless I've got several thousand Timothys out there, anointed and called and trained and ready for marching orders, my life and my ministry will be ended. To be a champion for God, I am convinced I've got to reproduce myself in others."

Dr. Jerry Falwell loves nothing better

than to participate in a young Timothy's newly formed church, He will often exert super-human effort to attend such functions. On one such occasion, Falwell sat on the stage of a school gymnasium watching a former LBC student, now the pastor of a newly formed church, present his welcoming remarks. Falwell sat back, beaming and obviously proud of this young pastor who was visible evidence of Falwell's "reproducing reproducers."

The particular evening occurred at the end of a long day which had begun about four that morning with a jet ride from Lynchburg to Lansing, Michigan, for an "I Love America" rally and continued with a luncheon for pastors and Christian school leaders. The Michigan trip had then been interrupted for a jet trip back to Lynchburg where Falwell, ever the pastor of his flock, officiated at a funeral. Because he had promised to attend the gathering at the gymnasium, and this commitment was to a former student, he flew back to Michigan to be at the meeting. But on that evening, pride in his "kid" overcame the fatigue which only became evident much later—after Falwell stood in the hot auditorium for about an hour after the service, graciously signing Bibles from the congregation, joking with the crowd, and offering a hand in friendship and encouragement.

Through the opening remarks, however, Dr. Falwell sat by beaming, listening to his former student's remarks, joining in the sing-

ing, accepting the key to the city, and, in general, acting just as proud as a father at his son's graduation. In a way, that is just what he was. A student had graduated into daily life, taking with him all the theory and education he had learned at Liberty Baptist College.

This scene is repeated for Jerry Falwell almost weekly. He is surrogate father for these students. He's a teacher in the practical aspects of life, a mentor in the field of ministership, and a confidant to discouraged or frightened kids. He shares their disappointments; he glories in their successes. They are a part of him, these youths who are trained and disciplined to go to "the uttermost parts of the earth," taking God's promises with them. They are Jerry Falwell's legacy to a spiritually starved world.

Falwell congratulating the LBC cheerleaders on a job well done.

*"A merry heart doeth good like a medicine
. . . and all things, whatsoever ye shall ask
in prayer, believing, ye shall receive"
(Prov. 17:22, Matt. 21:22).*

7

The Private Falwell

The door to the small private jet is closed, and all heads inside are bowed in prayer for safety before the plane taxies out to the runway. Now, high above the clouds of Virginia, on a return flight from an "I Love America" rally, the people of Jerry Falwell's team are, for the most part, tired from three days of little sleep and constant meetings and subdued from the tension of tight schedules. Don Norman, song leader of the team, is discussing with soloist Robbie Hiner changes and revisions in the lyrics of a song Robbie has just written. The photographer and security chief are discussing the day's activities and crowds. And Dr. Falwell is taking advantage of the quiet moment to attack some paperwork which has to be done.

Suddenly, Falwell reaches out a large fist and playfully punches Norman on the shoulder, then reaches over and nudges a ticklish member of the team right below the ribs, resulting in a loud, high-pitched squeal. The fatigue and the quiet of the moment before have gone, to be replaced by a camaraderie and relaxation broken by jokes, laughter, reminiscences of one day's blessings and hopes for the next. The punch and the nudge seem to have been some silent, yet physical, reminder to stay alive, to shake the fatigue.

Prayer and good humor: these are the moving forces of the private Jerry Falwell—the two qualities that dispel fear or fatigue and insure the success of God's ministry here on earth through this man.

Jerry Falwell's schedule is busy and full, and the man who has always been called a "prankster" seems to instinctively make use of good humor as a way to ease the tensions of himself and of others. His laugh is deep and ever ready to bubble over; and after forty-seven

Photo opposite: Dr. Jerry Falwell.

years, the lines of his face have deepened from the wide grin so characteristic of the man. His boyhood pranks are legendary to his friends; and even today, his antics continue in a good-natured manner which keeps family, friends, and team members on their toes and usually on their guard.

Twelve-year old boys seem to know what type of foolishness will make the little girls scream, and Jerry Falwell was no different. He just may have succeeded more often than most little boys. He was particularly fond of snakes, and they often accompanied him to school. He would stuff them down his shirt and climb aboard the school bus, clutching book and snake close to his chest. Once in his seat toward the back of the bus and directly behind a little girl, he'd take out the snake and drape it around the girl's neck. The bus, of course, would erupt in screaming students, some, usually little boys, watching in hysterics, and others, mostly little girls, valiantly trying to help unwind the snake from around the un-

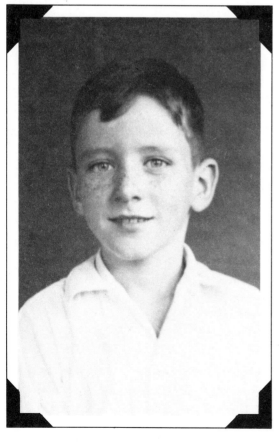

Jerry Falwell in the first grade.

lucky girl's neck. His daily morning foolishness completed, Falwell usually retrieved the snake and stuffed it back in its hiding place before the bus driver had time to get involved.

One day, however, the driver had heard enough and stopped the bus. Young Falwell grabbed the snake and stuffed it back down his shirt, but the driver still called, "Falwell, come up here!"

Falwell got up from the back of the bus and said, "Yes, Sir."

"Give me whatever you've got!"

"Yes, Sir," and with that, Jerry Falwell obediently pulled out that snake and handed it to the driver.

The bus driver recoiled quickly, hastily opened the door, and ejected both boy and snake from the bus.

If Falwell didn't find a snake on the way to school, he might pick up a rat, as he remembers doing one day. He grabbed a particularly large rat right in the middle of its back and continued into his Latin class. The Latin teacher had a habit of nibbling on cookies or crackers which she kept in her desk drawer. Falwell put the rat in that drawer.

Sure enough, during class, the teacher gave the students a writing project and opened her drawer to reach for a bite. The rat jumped out and right into her face. Unfortunately for Falwell, the poor woman fainted. The principal didn't have to ask who was responsible; he simply came down to the room and said, "Falwell, come with me!"

Snakes and rats are the tools of young boys, and when Dr. Falwell became a man, he put away such childish things. He turned to alligators. At least that was what his wife, Macel, found swimming in her bathtub one morning after her husband had returned from a trip to Florida.

Humor heals wounds; it breaks fatigue; it creates a bond between strangers and friends. Jerry Falwell uses it well, today in a more subtle way, as a reminder not to take himself or, sometimes, other people too seriously. In

"Most people take themselves too seriously. They can't laugh at themselves; they can't make a mistake and admit it without feeling they've compromised their leadership. People don't mind your being human."

fact, humor is a necessary tool in Falwell's ministries and in his life. He speaks of it: "Most people take themselves too seriously. They can't laugh at themselves; they can't make a mistake and admit it without feeling they've compromised their leadership. People don't mind your being human. Today, the tensions on everybody are such that a fellow who can't get people laughing, who can't laugh at himself, really can't attract the crowd, because you not only need to unwind, but you need to help other people unwind.

"I've always tried to use humor for this purpose, and I see now that it is necessary to be light. I feel that preachers who cannot really be personable and warm and make people happy are missing a chance to help others. At Thomas Road, there is never a service where there isn't some foolishness going on, when somebody isn't ribbing somebody else. And our people are like that in the work. Very little is totally serious until we get right down to the business of preaching the Word and trying to save souls."

In "preaching the Word and trying to save souls," Falwell is still good-natured; yet this is, indeed, the serious side of Falwell and often calls for the seriousness of prayer and meditation in the Scriptures.

The demands on the leader of as large and varied a ministry as Jerry Falwell's are great; however, he never seems to lose his patience or his graciousness toward people. After every speaking engagement, people crowd around him, pressing just to shake his hand, to have

him sign their Bibles or just to talk with him for a moment. Always, Falwell has the ready smile, the extended hand, and the attentive ear. Yet all human beings do tire and even ministers, at times, find that their own inner resources have been exhausted. In order to successfully minister to others, Jerry Falwell, through self-discipline and a daily regimen of prayer, makes certain that his spirit is constantly renewed by the Lord.

Before Falwell's conversion, he did have an impatience that was not always under complete control. If such things are inherited, Falwell may have come into this world with a quick temper. In looking back at his father's life, he says: "My father was a high-tempered man. Now that can be an asset if the temper is under the control of the Holy Spirit and we can direct it toward sin, toward Satan, toward injustice. But if my dad became angry with somebody, he would never forgive them. If he were for you, you couldn't do anything wrong; if he were against you, you couldn't do anything right.

"God gives everyone the ability to act or react; but to some of us, I think he gives a more flamboyant personality in that direction. Before I became a Christian I was quite high-tempered, but it would take a great deal to anger me. For instance, I would get upset when something really went wrong in athletics or when someone intentionally did something illegal or hurtful. I felt compelled to retaliate immediately.

"After my conversion, I found I still had

59

"You do not determine a man's greatness by his talent or by his wealth, as the world does, but rather by what it takes to discourage him."

that tendency, but I had dwelling in me the Holy Spirit who was fully able, if I was walking in the Spirit, to repress and control those emotions. I can't recall, since I became a Christian, ever being out of control in that way."

Through God's help, Falwell has learned to suppress any unkind actions or words which might have occurred during stress or fatigue. He has learned the warning signals when such times might occur; and to prevent them, he goes to the One who can soothe all stress and cause fatigue to flee. At these times, he takes advantage of a break in the schedule or postpones things for awhile and retreats to a quiet place for an extended time in prayer and in the Word. Falwell explains these times: "It's very easy to get so caught up in this work that you get into a whirlwind of activity and dry up spiritually in the process. It can happen every other day, but as long as you're alert to it and do not allow it to persist, as long as you make adjustments, it's not an abnormal thing. There is nothing wrong with running out of fuel; there is, however, something wrong with not refueling."

Refueling is a daily necessity and Falwell begins his with Bible reading and prayer the first thing every morning, usually about an hour before the rest of the family rises. There is another opportunity for private meditations about three days a week when he is in the soundproof broadcast studio. He finds that the time before the broadcast begins is an excellent time to take advantage of the complete quiet to study and prepare for the day. He also takes advantage of times alone in his car. Often, when he is troubled by a particularly heavy burden, Falwell climbs into his car and drives, finding this an excellent time alone in which to talk to God about the problems.

As might be expected with a large ministry, there are daily problems, sometimes small, sometimes large. Spiritual leader to thousands, Jerry Falwell knows how necessary it is for him to give his problems to the only one who can do anything about them.

No one, even those who know him best and are constantly close to him, remembers ever seeing Falwell discouraged or down. This is not because he has never had extensive burdens; it's merely a reflection of the viewpoint Falwell holds concerning discouragement, a belief that, through self-discipline, he has been able to put into practice. From the pulpit he has discussed discouragement, and his words describing the successful could certainly pertain to him also: "Discouragement is always of the devil. Whatsoever is not of faith is sin. Faith is believing God no matter what the environment dictates. Discouragement is believing the circumstances and the environment no matter what God has said. Champions must learn to conquer their emotions. Conquerors and champions and victors must never succumb to discouragement. I often tell our young people here, you do not determine a man's greatness by his talent or by his wealth, as the world does, but rather by what it takes to discourage him."

Falwell simply does not allow himself to become discouraged. He has a schedule for refueling which has become a precise and

Photo opposite: Falwell working at his desk in the church offices. LBC emblem is hanging at back.

daily habit.

"I make it a practice in the morning to go into my study with a pencil and pad as though I were sitting down with a worker across the desk. I have my Bible reading first, which I feel is God's way of talking to me. Very often, as I go through the Bible sequentially, the Lord will address, through a particular passage, the burdens and problems that are in my mind and heart already. Then, when I begin to pray, I will write down the things I am praying about, the concerns the Lord lays on my heart, so they will be there the next morning. Obviously they gather. The specific things are decisions that must be made that day. The next morning, I sort them out, but pray about them right there and really try to obey the Scriptures, to submit everything to the Lord in prayer and thanksgiving. If we have unhappy things we have to do, sometimes I may find it necessary to spend a lot of time there.

"During the day, I find that a good time to pray is when driving a car, because I'm alone then. I spend the time talking to God. It is my way of bringing all my burdens to the Lord and nobody else. I don't take home any problems, even to Macel, because she doesn't need those extra problems. I try to deal with them and take them to the Lord. When I come home, I try to be home. Macel is not even aware of ninety-five percent of the problems we face here, ever. Things of that nature, particularly heavy burdens, she couldn't help with, and they would just be unnecessary burdens on her."

Jerry Falwell has developed the ability to privately give his burdens to God and be able to walk away, knowing the Lord will work them out. He does this not only because it is Scriptural, but because it is also a matter of common sense. He speaks of this ability: "Discouragement is contagious. There's nothing wrong with having an intimate prayer partner; that's what pastors and counselors are for, and strong spiritual friends. There is a danger, however, in dwelling upon and discussing problems and burdens with people so that they become your burden bearers instead of

Jerry Falwell often seeks privacy and solitude in his car and uses this opportunity to talk over his problems with God.

Falwell and Dr. Sumner Wemp pray
before services at Thomas Road Church.

the Lord, and at the same time, your problems depress them. They cannot do much except pray for you and you can communicate that need without making a big thing out of it. Scripture teaches that we are to take our burdens to the Lord and leave them there. When a burden returns, and it will, we are to go back to the Lord and stay with Him and talk over all facets of it with Him, going back to Him until the burden has been removed to Him. If and when that need returns, we are to go right back again and repeat the process.

"I can usually tell when I'm physically tired and spiritually tired, because at those times, I'm less under control. It's a good warning to me that I've been doing too much and I need to fall back and get refueled spiritually. The persons who are victims of their emotions are generally not spending enough time with the Lord, because the fruit of the Spirit in Galatians 5:22-23 is love, joy, peace, long-suffering, then gentleness, goodness, faith,

meekness; the last one is temperance, or self-control. So it is definitely the fruit of the Spirit for anybody to have self-control if he will walk in the Spirit. When I'm not in the Spirit is when I'm most likely to react in a way that is not Christlike. I use that as a flag; and when I see it beginning to happen, I know that I need to get a little bit closer to the Lord."

Jerry Falwell has a schedule which would exhaust a man half his age and constant pressures and problems which would rival those of any business executive. Falwell's burdens are those of life and death—people's souls often hang in the balance. Yet he recognizes the fact that he alone cannot solve the problems, and neither he nor anyone here on earth can "save" a soul. Falwell is God's messenger and administrator. When the problems weigh heavily, Jerry Falwell lets off steam through laughter and takes his burdens to the Lord. And he leaves them there, for God is the only one who can supply all our needs.

"If my people, which are called by my name, shall humble themselves, and pray, and seek my face, and turn from their wicked ways; then will I hear from heaven, and will forgive their sin, and will heal their land" (2 Chron. 7:14).

8

Decade of Destiny

The "Decade of Destiny" is a term Jerry Falwell often uses to describe the 1980s. The history of the world is replete with examples of nations which had become strong, then weakened and ultimately failed. Falwell (and many other people) believes America is now entering a crisis period which may result in a similar downfall.

The reason that the 1980s loom as a precarious decade in terms of survival is that, at the threshold to this decade, the country is suffering multiple moral breakdowns, some of which have occurred before but never all at once. The nation is experiencing a decline in military preparedness, the loss of traditional moral values, a disregard for family solidarity, a turn from the discipline of basic education, and, perhaps foremost, a dearth of capable leaders.

Falwell believes the problem is so great

and so serious that it is the reason for his patriotic rallies and a recurring theme from his pulpit. He says: "During the next ten years, unlike any ten years in the history of this country, the nation must face the fact that America is militarily inferior and very likely to remain so because we don't have the commitment of government to do anything about it. That means we are going to become increasingly more subservient and be subjected to the bullying tactics of the Soviet Union. The Irans and the Afghanistans are going to multiply, because it has become obvious we cannot do anything about them. These kinds of situations are going to be arising in South America, Central America, Mexico, and even in Quebec; and we are going to find ourselves, as a nation, very close to losing our freedom, if in fact we don't. That has never been true before.

"The humanists have successfully gained

Falwell accepts the opportunity to discuss his views on the state of Israel with Prime Minister Begin.

control of government and the schools. Education of students in America at the primary, secondary, and university levels is controlled by the humanists, so that all of the moral values which have been so precious to this country, to our forefathers and to every generation, are beginning to disappear. It's a matter of fact that, as hard as we fight, without a dramatic turnaround precipitated by a spiritual awakening unlike anything the country has ever known, the family may be nonexistent by the end of this decade, except in the older groups which are fading away.

"I see the 1980s as a Decade of Destiny. We have always had on the horizon strong men who were ready to take the helm at every strata—government, law, business, education, and the ministry—at the right moment and lead the people in the right direction. Today, I don't see them anywhere. I ask people all the time who are the ten greatest men in America, and few can think of that many great leaders. I ask them, 'Who is the man if we could put him in the White House who could lead the country out of these crises?' And few can think of one name. There are a few Jesse Helms around the country that are looked on as men of impeccable character, and who are decisive and will do the right thing every time.

"We have to pay the price for freedom; and if we're not willing to pay the price, God will give us what we want. He repeatedly sold His people into bondage. The book of Judges is the story of one bondage after another. When the people cried out for mercy, God sent a deliverer. For a short time they walked with God and really honored the Lord; then they forgot Him, and once again their nation fell. I think our country is now at the point where we could fall. I don't think that is alarmism; I

66

think that's a fact, unless we repent now. The question is, then, if we repent and get right with God, will God bring us out? I really don't know."

This is the ominous and frightening view of the country today as Falwell sees it. Jerry Falwell, however, believes implicitly that God can solve the problems, in fact, *only* God can cure the nation's illness. He takes this belief from the promise given in 2 Chronicles 7:14: *"If my people, which are called by my name, shall humble themselves, and pray, and seek my face, and turn from their wicked ways; then will I hear from heaven, and will forgive their sin, and will heal their land."* Falwell clings to this promise as the only hope for the nation.

The question was, however, how does one person, who believes he has the ultimate answer to the country's salvation, convince the people to collectively call upon God? Falwell, who had trusted God to build a church from thirty-five people in a bottling plant to a membership of seventeen thousand, who had turned a thirty-minute daily radio spot into the most watched television ministry in the world, and who had built a respected college from a handful of students meeting in houses, had not a doubt that it *could* be done. He just had to figure out *how.*

Actually, that wasn't as difficult as he had first thought. If he were going to build a political organization as Jerry Falwell, private citizen, he would go to someone who had already built one, such as a Christian politician. Falwell explains: "I had made a study the last several years on how we could reverse the national trend toward destruction. I've always known that prayer was a part of it, preaching was a part of it, building churches was a part

President Sadat and Dr. Falwell enjoying a moment of levity during serious discussions on the Middle East situation.

67

Elected officials often join Dr. Falwell at the "I Love America" rallies. From left to right: U.S. Rep. Robert Dornan (Calif.), Sen. Gordon Humphrey (N.H.), Sen. John Warner (Va.), Sen. Paul Laxalt (Nev.), and Sen. Jesse Helms (N.C.).

of it; but there was a missing link. Why, with the tremendous moral majority we have in this country, does the government keep moving away from traditional moral values? The fact is, we don't have our people locked into the process. So then the question was, how can we begin to do that?

"I decided I would talk with good Christian politicians at a high level of the nation and have them teach me how to do it. I talked with about a dozen top political leaders in the country, top-level lobbyists, organizations in Washington, many of whom believed the opposite of what I believed. I talked with them anyway to find out how they got things done. I learned that the answer is organization.

"It's just the same as the way we build a church, no difference. We have over one thousand teachers and workers in our Sunday School at Thomas Road Baptist Church. Those thou-sand Sunday School teachers are out doing all the work that makes Sunday School a success whether I'm out of town or in town. It just goes right on. I learned that's what they do in politics, from the precinct level up, not from the top down."

Armed with the knowledge of how to organize a political organization, Falwell set out to do just that. He set up a national board and an executive council. In each of the fifty states, a state chairman was appointed, one of the most respected pastors of the state who was interested in joining the cause. The chairman functions as the spokesman for that state and heads the organization's state office. This does not conflict with the pastor's ministry because it is a volunteer position and doesn't violate tax codes. These state offices are more and more becoming important clearinghouses in the dissemination of information on state and national political issues.

Falwell dubbed this political-moral organization he founded the "Moral Majority" because he believes that the majority of Americans hold the same basic moral ideas as the Ten Commandments, whether they be Christian or nonbeliever, Democrat or Republican, rich or poor. He strongly believes that it is a liberal, radical, vocal minority who have been influencing the government in the recent past and who now provide the image by which other countries see us. It is to this "moral majority" that Falwell speaks, and on them hinges his belief that the country can be saved.

The Moral Majority's primary purpose is to organize people from all walks of life and from all religious persuasions who are pro-life, pro-family, pro-moral, and pro-American in order to create a climate that makes it easy for politicians to do what is right. Falwell believes that the moral condition of a nation is usually a reflection of the spiritual condition of the churches in that nation. The Moral Majority was begun to provide a vehicle of communication for pastors throughout the country.

The Moral Majority is also active in lobbying, and in 1979 was instrumental in the adoption of the Dornan and Ashbrook Amendments to the Internal Revenue Appropriations Bill

When the Falwell team visits a state capitol with a rally, Jerry Falwell often has the opportunity to discuss contemporary moral issues with the governor of the state as he is doing here with Gov. Carroll of Kentucky.

for 1980. These amendments restrain the IRS from using any of their funds to investigate, harass, or in any way involve themselves in private schools. This is a twelve-month reprieve, which means the battle for the freedom of the Christian schools is not yet won, but the Moral Majority is making its influence felt by legislators.

The growing political clout of this organization is evident. Jerry Falwell has come to be accepted by such world leaders as Prime Minister Begin and President Sadat as unofficial spokesman for a large segment of the American people. Falwell is on amicable terms with these governments and considers Begin and Sadat to be personal friends. The Middle East is of extreme importance to the Moral Majority because Falwell believes strongly in the continued defense of Israel.

Throughout history, the nations who have not upheld the rights of the Jews have fallen. For the basis of their continued defense, Falwell again returns to the Bible. When God told Abraham He would make of him a great nation, He also said, *"I will bless them that bless thee, and curse him that curseth thee"* (Gen. 12:3). Falwell adds, "If Hitler could rise up from hell today, he would say, 'Amen' to that."

This is the reason Falwell is willing and delighted to have the opportunity to speak with foreign leaders, such as Prime Minister Begin to whom he read the above passage. He has also discussed the situation with President Sadat and read him the same passage from Genesis, explaining that this passage is from our Book, the Word of God. To Sadat, Falwell added that the Bible also records God's words, "Egypt have I loved."

That he would face a world leader like Sadat, read him what probably would be an unpopular passage from the Bible and then take the time to explain why he believes as he does says a lot about Jerry Falwell. If Falwell believes he is right and has the truth, and concerning the defense of Israel he certainly does believe that, he tells that truth to all who listen, however unpopular it might be. In discussing the idea of what some might see as unwise outspokenness, Falwell states: "If you're telling the truth, you can tell it the same way every place. If you're telling it right, you don't have to remember what you said, and if you don't change for political convenience, you don't have to be concerned about what you said the last time." This dedication to telling the truth has gained Jerry Falwell the respect of leaders everywhere.

With the growing recognition of its political clout, during the decade of the eighties, the Moral Majority should be a strong political force in this country, but it will never be a political party. Dr. Falwell rules this possibility out completely and explains why: "We don't need a third party. What we really need is to mobilize and inform the moral majority in America regarding the real issues which will determine whether America 'deserves to survive.' Solomon said in Proverbs 14:34 *'Righteousness exalteth a nation: but sin is a reproach to any people.'* America does have economic, energy, and military crises. But our basic problem is a moral crisis. If America can be brought back to the biblical, moral principles which have caused God to make this the greatest nation on earth, God can once more bless America; and the churches in America have a spiritual and material responsibility toward the whole world. Only in an environment of freedom can America's churches evangelize the world. America has a responsibility to protect Israel. The Moral Majority is organizing rapidly to help America fulfill her role."

Members of the Moral Majority encompass all faiths. Falwell calls the basis of their unity one "not of theology, but one of citizenship. We've been able to get these people to join together for the mutual benefit of all of us. We must forget our personal differences and work out a coalition and fight together for the same design and the same purpose."

Members come together who are of various persuasions and are very committed in some areas, only nominally committed in other areas; but they are all willing to fight together for a united front. If there is a moral majority in the country, they have not been vocal in the past because they were not united. That has changed. They are now organized and expect to be heard lobbying, informing, and educating the public to elect candidates and pass laws.

Falwell has no plans to enter politics and, perhaps surprisingly, does not look for a theologically correct political candidate to endorse. The Moral Majority and Jerry Falwell are principle oriented. The Moral Majority believes that God blesses biblical principles. Falwell has stated that if he had to choose between a Christian who disagreed with these moral issues and a nonbeliever who agreed with them, he would vote for the nonbeliever. And why not? Jerry Falwell believes God is sovereign and will direct that person's course based on the prayers and petitions of His people.

The last thing Falwell and the Moral Majority want to see is the emergence of a state church. On this subject, he states: "I am very much opposed to a state church. A prime example of the result of any church leader running a government is the situation in Iran right now. I'm not saying any Christian leader would ever be like the Ayatollah, but the ultimate result would be the same; it could result in a total abolition of religious rights for everybody.

"We would fight for Madalyn O'Hair's right to practice atheism, because the same laws that give her that right protect us. I've found myself on the same side as Madalyn O'Hair on a lot of issues. I agree that the government can give no favors to the church and the church cannot run the government, but the church should exert a moral influence on the government and create a moral conscience in the land that makes the government do right—not because they have to, but because it is the right thing to do. That is the difference between a dictatorship and an influential church. The church in America needs to become influential in its teaching and holy living, and we need to exert that influence in a legal way and train our people to do that. This would result in a candidate stopping to think, 'Hey, I have to keep my own family in order and set a good example. I'm going to have to take the right stand on these moral issues.' He won't even consider going off in left field in those areas because he won't get elected."

Although Falwell does not believe in a state church, he makes a distinction between God and church. Most rallies will find him saying: "Separation of church and state is one thing. Separation of God and state is another thing. Pornography, homosexuality, and a number of other moral issues that have now become political issues do not preempt pastors from speaking out on them. The Roman Catholic Church has never stopped speaking out on them, which is to their credit. In the Evangelical world, we have allowed people to browbeat us into believing that politics and religion do not mix. I think if politics becomes our priority, of course, it's a violation. Our number one purpose is a spiritual one, but if we don't keep the country open and free, then we're not going to have the right to preach. So all we're doing is taking a little segment of time out of our total time structure to go outside and fight to have the right to go back inside and preach."

There are those who believe God will work his purposes regardless of man's involvement. Falwell believes God is, of course, sovereign, but cites biblical history to prove that man's responsibility and irresponsibility have

> *"When it comes down to the destruction of human life (abortion), the home, the family, and when it comes down to pornography on the newsstands or obscenity on the television set, that's where the preacher's role is. I believe the preacher's role is to keep this country fit for our children's children yet to come. That is where we ought to fight—and without any apology."*

played a large part in God's actions: "There is a verse in Matthew where Jesus said, *'It must needs be that offences come; but woe to that man by whom the offence cometh'* (18:7). Christians have a responsibility, and the sovereignty of God must always be balanced by the responsibility of man. There are two sides to the coin and unless we see both sides, we wreck God's program.

"God didn't want Israel to have a king; but they demanded a king to be like other nations. So God gave them Saul, a wicked king, who drove them in the ground. It didn't have to be, but that's what they wanted. I think God wants people to be free. But we have to want to be free to the extent that we will wake up to the fact that the government is not always speaking for the American people, that the foreign policy is not always reflective of what the people want—in *many* cases, it is not. And the World Council of Churches, more often than not, is not voicing the sentiments of the American people, so other nations are beginning to disregard them as a non-authoritative voice. Those nations are asking now for others to come forward."

The Moral Majority and Dr. Falwell are coming out to speak for moral Americans; but Falwell is quick to point out that the issues they are concerned with are limited in scope.

"There are many things they are discussing in Washington that I believe are out of my area. But when they are dealing with freedom, morality, the family, or the home, I believe a preacher has not just a right, but an obligation, to fight. In strictly political and economic areas, all of us have our views. But those areas are not where I think the country will live or die. I think the politicians on both sides have their points; they are working for the welfare of the country.

"But when it comes down to the destruction of human life (abortion), the home, the family, and when it comes down to pornography on the newsstands or obscenity on the television set, that's where the preacher's role is. I believe the preacher's role is to keep this country fit for our children's children yet to come. That is where we ought to fight—and without any apology."

The Decade of Destiny is upon us. Jerry Falwell knows that the ultimate failure or success of this country is laid upon the shoulders of her people. He believes the answer is God's intervention, but whether it will come is dependent upon the fight left in Americans. Two hundred years ago, Benjamin Franklin, upon leaving the Continental Congress, was asked what kind of government the new country had. He responded, "You have a republic, if you can keep it." Jerry Falwell, under God's banner, has entered the battle to keep it.

Photo opposite: With flags flying behind him, Falwell speaks out on contemporary moral issues from the capitol steps.

"Go ye therefore, and teach all nations, baptizing them in the name of the Father, and of the Son, and of the Holy Ghost: teaching them to observe all things whatsoever I have commanded you: and, lo, I am with you alway, even unto the end of the world" (Matt. 28:19, 20).

9

The Vision of Jerry Falwell

The great coach Vince Lombardi, whom Jerry Falwell is fond of quoting, once said, "Winning is not a sometime thing. It's an all the time thing. You don't win once in awhile; you don't do things right once in awhile. You do them right all the time. Winning is a habit. Unfortunately, so is losing. There is no room for second place."

From the time Jerry Falwell was playing on the athletic field or graduating as valedictorian of his high school class or rooting for the New York Yankees, the most successful baseball team ever, he has had a drive to succeed—to win. That doesn't mean he has always reached his goal, for there have been setbacks and losses. But somehow, in Jerry Falwell's life, even a loss can be a small victory; for there are lessons to be learned from losses. It is the *attitude* about winning and losing which is important to the final goal.

"I think one can win humbly as well as lose humbly," says Dr. Falwell, "and it's far better. There is a time for losing. It really doesn't matter what you're doing; there's a time when you're learning to do it. But I think a Christian has to develop a winning personality—a personality and a disposition toward winning. It's a mental thing and you have to set your goals toward that. If you think that way, ultimately, with God's grace, you're going to do what you do better than anyone else. I think you will. But it takes discipline. Most outstanding athletes are not outstanding because they have more innate ability than the guys they beat, but just because they put themselves to the task. They have the discipline of training that the other guy doesn't. They run longer, work harder, and pay the necessary price to achieve their goal."

When Falwell began Thomas Road Bap-

"Winning is getting up earlier than the other guy and going to bed later; and it's working harder in between. I personally don't think anybody has ever hurt himself by working hard."

tist Church, he worked longer and harder than most. He set goals for attendance and practiced the self-discipline necessary for attaining each goal, until reaching his goals became a habit. He continued this practice of setting definite goals for the schools, the outreach ministries, and the political organization. He tells of the necessity of goal-setting: "When I was starting Thomas Road Church, to overcome any possibility of laziness or slothfulness, without anyone knowing it, I set goals for myself, such as, we are going to have five hundred regularly attending here by a certain date. Preacher friends of mine who had comparable ministries, or were a little ahead of us, would have contests with us and we would really go after it. The people wouldn't be much involved in it, but it would be just for ourselves, for the purpose of disciplining ourselves to excellence, to reaching more people. There's nothing wrong with reaching more people as long as it's not numbers for numbers' sake or for the purpose of an ego trip. It's certainly not wrong as long as you want to reach people for Christ and for the purpose of developing in their lives the qualities God wants them to have.

"The reason we want to win is to do a better job for the Lord, to bring more honor to Him, and to help more people. That's honorable. If it is done so that I can be promoted and glorified, then God won't bless that; God won't honor it and it will come to nothing. In athletics, the ministry, or whatever career a person is pursuing, he has to set his own goals. Winning is getting up earlier than the other guy and going to bed later; and it's working harder in between. I personally don't think anybody has ever hurt himself by working hard."

The primary purpose of a minister, then, is not just to have a huge church membership, nor is it to have his face constantly on television or in the press. And this is not Falwell's purpose. The need to reach people, to fill the pews on Sunday morning, or to send his message via television is simply a means of reaching a much larger goal. And that is the ultimate vision of Jerry Falwell. The need to win, to reach people, even the need to help keep this country free are all only supportive to the primary purpose of Jerry Falwell.

In speaking of churches, Falwell has stated that a church's success lies not in its wealth, nor in its large membership, but "in winning souls. It is in bringing people to Jesus. It is in trying to reach everybody and in believing that Christ died not for a handful, or a chosen, select few, but that He died for the world, died for every Chinese, every Russian, for every American, for every Canadian, for every European. He died for all men."

The battle for men's souls is the ultimate fight; and, in this battle, to use a phrase from Lombardi, "There is no room for second place." Falwell is in the business of soul-winning, and the result is either a life in Christ or without Him. Jerry Falwell's vision is that same one given two thousand years ago: "That vision has never changed from the moment God gave it to those on the Mount of Olives when He said, *'Go ye therefore . . . in the name*

76

Photo opposite: In each capital city, the crowd gathers to hear Falwell speak on the issues vital to the survival of this country.

of the Father, and of the Son, and of the Holy Ghost.' That's enlistment into the local church. *'Teaching them to observe all things whatsoever I have commanded you.'* That is reproducing reproducers, that is, teaching them to go out and do likewise. Win them to Jesus, enlist them in the army, train them to go out and do the same thing. And He said, if you will do that, if you will carry out that three-pronged commission called world evangelization, *'Lo, I am with you alway, even unto the end of the world.'*

"The promise of God's presence and God's power, God's provision, is upon those and those only who are under the mandate, personally having caught the vision, to give the Gospel to the world."

What has made Falwell unique among ministers is his absolute total commitment to God, coupled with unfailing belief and knowledge of the omnipotence of God. Jerry Falwell dreams impossible dreams and trusts in God to fulfill them if it is His will. Falwell begins small, as in the case of the original thirty-five church members; but gradually, as God unfolds His plan, Falwell sees the larger possibilities. He explains this process: "We're often asked, did you envision twenty years ago what God would do? And the answer without hesitation on my part is 'no.' For vision grows with activity. As God works through you and as miracles happen, faith increases and vision enlarges. If God is in something, it's never static or stagnant. If God is in something, it's on the move. When something is standing still, it isn't God's fault. For God is on the move. He has only one gear and that is upward and forward. There is no reverse in His transmission. There is no panic button near His throne. Everything is under control; it's all going according to His program. God plans for us to get His Gospel out to every creature, and we've got to have the vision to do it. Now that leads me to say, if you're going to be a winner, you've got to be willing to gamble. I don't mean the kind of gambling that's done at racetracks. I'm talking abut the kind of gambling that the Bible speaks of: gambling on the integrity of God, gambling on the promises of the Book. *'My God shall supply*

The first "I Love America" rally was held on the steps of the nation's Capitol in Washington, D.C.

78

Frequent jet trips offer Dr. Falwell moments of quiet in which to prepare speeches, read, or refuel from the Word of God.

all your needs according to His riches in glory by Christ Jesus.'"

Jerry Falwell's life has been a continuing trust in God to supply the necessities and a commitment on his part to "keep on the move." From the need to preach the Gospel in Lynchburg grew a burning desire to reach the world. Jerry Falwell spreads the Gospel by radio, by television, by word of mouth. He spreads the Gospel through young people trained to go out and start churches and through athletic programs. Jerry Falwell would go anywhere and try almost any method to reach the world with the message that Jesus Christ died to save the world. He has said of his world ministry: "I thank God for this television ministry. I thank God for radio. We're reaching people that maybe we'll never know about until we get on the other side. But I believe we should pray that God will put their hands on the dial and help them turn those sets on and hear. That's why I never preach without talking about the death, burial, and resurrection of Christ. I never want to assume that every viewer is a Christian, because there may be just that one time a person tunes

in who will never do it again, who may be dead tomorrow, who will hear how to be saved."

The television and radio ministry are only a part of Falwell's world vision. His goal is to reach everyone with the message—some way, sometime. "We need to catch the vision," he says, "that there has to be a way to tell the world. There has to be a way to do it. You say it will take hundreds of millions of dollars to do it. Well, then let's just raise it. Let's just trust God for it. It will take thousands of young people. Well, then, let's bring them here and train them. Whatever it takes, let's just do it.

"I think God is big enough. God made everything that's on this planet. And if we had the capability of seeing out yonder into God's universe, past what the telescopes show, past what the textbooks relate, we would find out that this universe is just as infinite as is God; we haven't seen the rim yet. The same is true about what God wants to do on this earth."

In spite of talk of world vision and dreams of infinite possibilities, Falwell's message is always the same—the simple, yet life-changing message, given by Jesus Christ centuries ago: "In every message," Rev. Falwell says, "I try to give the Gospel. Regardless of how simple and repetitious the message may seem, it is the only message that gets people into a successful life. The Gospel is that Christ died for our sins, according to the Scriptures. He was buried and on the third day He rose from the dead, according to the Scriptures. The death, the burial, the resurrection of Jesus Christ is the Gospel. And a man who believes the Gospel and trusts the shed blood of Jesus as the full payment of his sin debt is redeemed. He is washed in that blood; he is, in the Bible term, saved; he becomes a child of God."

Jerry Falwell, for all his activities and his organizations, in spite of his control of large organizations with huge budgets, still remains a child of God, dedicated to the task of winning souls to Christ. That is why Falwell is out to "win" and makes no apologies for this desire. He knows he has the answer to man's salvation and is obligated to spread the word. It is not his life's work, it is his life. And he will continue on the move toward that day when his work here will be finished. Toward that time, Falwell spoke: "I firmly believe any man's finest hour, his greatest fulfillment to all he holds dear, is that moment when he has worked his heart out in a good cause and lies exhausted on the field of battle, victorious. There is no excuse for anything but victory. One day we will hear Him say, 'well done, thou good and faithful servant.'

"If you're going to be a singer, be a champion singer. If you're going to be a bus captain, be the best bus captain in God's world. If you're going to be a preacher, be a champion preacher. If you're going to be a mother and a housewife, be the best one in your town. In a world that is attempting to reduce all men to the ordinary, we find it a time that calls for extraordinary men, giants, unusual men."

The Apostle Paul said, *"If God be for us, who can be against us?"* If a person were to truly believe this, make it a daily and constant thought, he could indeed move mountains. Jerry Falwell is such a man. He has been called phenomenal, and he has been praised for his successes. He has been called a prophet; he's called pastor. What he is, is a man on the move for Christ.

In a small-town church some twenty-eight years ago, Jerry Falwell came face to face with his Savior. He has never doubted since that time. This is why he can forge ahead, moving those mountains and building on those dreams. That is why his vision becomes reality. That is why he never becomes totally discouraged and his failures are only temporary setbacks. Jerry Falwell is confident that God will not fail; He will not desert His people who continue to call upon His name.

Falwell has put on the whole armor of God. His faith is grounded in the reality of God and the experience that God accomplishes what He has promised. Thus armed, he plunges into the battle that is raging for men's souls, and Falwell, in the pulpit, often sounds like a man equipped for the battle. "The man who wins the battle," he says, "is the fellow who is knocked down nine times but gets up ten. He's the fellow who will not accept defeat, who will never learn to sound retreat, who will never turn back. That is the reason why, in Ephesians 6, God didn't provide any armor for the hind-parts; He never planned for us to turn around. Upward and onward, and the gates of hell shall not keep us out."

What makes Jerry Falwell an extraordinary man "in a world that is attempting to reduce all men to the ordinary?" He is a man with a passion for souls. He is a man who burns with the desire that all people will hear the words: *"For God so loved the world, that He gave His only begotten Son, that whosoever believeth in Him should not perish, but have everlasting life."* He is a man who is burdened with the responsibility to tell this message to as many as will listen, so that on some glorious day, Jerry Falwell will hear the words, "Well done, thou good and faithful servant."